Teach Yourself
SPANISH
Level One

A complete Spanish course with Audio
Dr. Yeral E. Ogando

Teach Yourself Spanish - Level One
© 2017 by Dr. Yeral E. Ogando
Publisher: Christian Translation LLC
Printed in the USA
Cover Design by SAL media

ISBN 13: 978-1-946249-04-3
ISBN 10: 1-946249-04-1

1. Language Learning 2. Spanish Language

DEDICATION:

This book is dedicated to the Unique and forever-lasting person who has always been there for me, no matter how stubborn I am:
GOD

I also want to dedicate this work to Sharon A. Lavy, who has given me the push I needed to write this book and to YOU (the reader), because you have taken the moment to read this incredible story and without you I would not have been here.
You all have a special place in my heart.
Always.

ACKNOWLEDGMENTS:

Gratitude to my Lord God for giving me the opportunity to write this book; Teach Yourself Spanish, dedicated to God above all, then to my daughters Yeiris & Tiffany, without them, this book would not be possible.

I also want to dedicate this work to all of you, who want to succeed in life and special to Gladys de Contreras, who has helped me through the process of getting the final edition and Franklin Guerra Castro for his talented voice in the audio.

This book has been inspired by all of you, thus providing you with an easy and comprehensive tool to learn the language quickly.

I encourage you to study the content of this book and you will see positive results in short time.

God bless you all

Dios les bendiga

Dr. Yeral E. Ogando

www.aprendeis.com

Table of Contents

Introduction

I have published this method for you to learn this language in a very quick and comprehensive way.

I kindly ask you to take 20 minutes of your time on a daily basis without interruption, so you can concentrate and digest the content of this work.

One of the biggest challenges in learning is to be a Self-Taught person, in other words, learn by yourself, it requires lots of discipline and dedication in your study. To study a full hour every day would make you feel tired and bored very quickly, that's why I recommend to you a minimum of 20 minutes per day and a maximum of 40 minutes per day, therefore, you will be achieving better results.

I wish you good luck in this amazing trip to the world of learning, and remember "Be shameless to speak."

Yeral Ogando
www.aprendeis.com

Before starting

Some people think and even say that you do not need to study the grammar of a language to learn it well. I humbly disagree with them. The non-grammar method could work with children, who have their minds ready for anything that you might feed them with; they have no worries, jobs, problems, so they are ready for it, but for adults with all our worries, responsibilities and most of the time, tired from work; it simply does not work. Our minds are already saturated with all kinds of stuff, so we need a way to really learn the language. After learning more than 10 languages, I have managed to master them and learn them very quickly because I have learned the pattern and short cuts for each language. I have also seen in my many years of teaching experience that you cannot learn a foreign language very well, if you don't know your own language. Thus, as you will see, you will learn your own language while studying a foreign language. This method is about recognizing and learning how to use the patterns on each grammar point.

I do not want you to learn words or phrases by heart, on the contrary, I want you to take your time and learn slowly by understanding each grammar point that I explain in this book. Your challenge is to recognize the patterns that I am teaching you. Once you recognize them and understand the structure of the language, you will improve your learning and speaking skills at a tremendous speed. Once again, pay close attention to the patterns, learn them, study them and then build your own Spanish world and vocabulary.

I am giving you the perfect tool to learn Spanish. You will be surprised to see how fast you can learn to recognize words. The texts in this book are up to date and modern Spanish for this generation, so be ready to improve your skills.

If you still have not downloaded your MP3 Audio files, check our BONUS PAGE for the DOWNLOAD.

I recommend that you always read aloud, so you can listen to yourself and compare the pronunciation with the one in the MP3 Audio. If you have any issues with the pronunciation, remember to check the **Pronunciation Chart.**

Teach Yourself Spanish is a powerful method that combines everyday conversation with real people, through grammar drills along with a vocabulary after every section. Pay close attention to the way people speak.

Grammar Explanations is a section that you need to make sure to understand and digest before moving to the next section. This book has been created to serve as a conversational and grammar at the same time. I have explained in details how to use the grammar in everyday conversation to help you master the language.

Do not forget that it is more effective to study a few minutes a day than to attempt to study a big portion occasionally. Your concentration will be best taken advantage of with 20 minutes of daily study.

Steps on how to use this book for better results

Go to the *BONUS* page for the instructions on how to download the MP3 Audio files. That is your first step. Your best companion and tool "the *AUDIO* file".

Lesson 1 will teach you everything about the alphabet, reading and writing Spanish. Work on lesson one along with the Audio to master the sounds and pronunciation. Take notes of any new words or phrase that you do not understand very well. Once you finish your reading and jotting down the new words and phrases, take a few minutes to review these new words and phrases.

Read the reading for each lesson aloud and try to understand the general meaning of the reading text. You do not need to understand every single word, you just need to have a general idea.

Now you can view the Vocabulary section underneath the reading. Locate the words or phrases that you do not fully understand. Learn them by heart. You will also find remarks and notes indicating pages number where you can learn more about any structure that is not for this unit. Pay close attention to these remarks on the *Word List.*

Now, you are ready to listen the MP3 audio. Make sure you play the MP3 and listen to the pronunciation of the native speakers. Get the gist of the pronunciation and practice it. If possible, try to imitate the pronunciation for any possible word or phrase that you are not sure. Listen to the MP3 audio as many times as possible.

Once you master the **Words List** for this lesson,

you can now move to the **Grammar** section, stated by

sign. Pay close attention to the words with the **Grammar** symbol. Review them in the text.

You are ready to move to the *A little bit more* section. In this section you will find list of phrases and / or new vocabularies to increase your learning skills. Make sure to learn them very well.

I have created a *Knowledge Base* section, where you will find basic information for each country where Spanish is the official language. Since there are 22 countries with Spanish as their official language, you will find a *Knowledge Base* covering the 22 countried on each lesson.

Your final and no less important section is "*Bible Verse*". I have included a Bible verse for each lesson, so you can conclude each lesson with a blessing and a Word from God to your heart. I have learned that there is no better resource to increase your learning skills and vocabulary than the "*Bible*". Try it and you will find words for every situation, occasion and time.

Make sure to repeat these steps over and over again until you master each lesson. Do not go to the next section if you have not mastered previous one. You MUST be sure you master each lesson before moving on. Your success will depend on following these steps.

Symbols And Abbreviations

Audio Symbol: This indicates that the MP3 Audio download is needed for this section

Dialogue Symbol: This indicates dialogue

Grammar Symbol: This indicates grammar explanations.

A little More Symbol: This indicates we have added a little more information to the lesson.

Lesson 1
Spanish Alphabet – Alfabeto Español

The Spanish alphabet consists of 27 letters. The Spanish language is quite easy to pronounce since most letters only have one sound. In Spanish it is very important to know the alphabet and their combinations, because you will be able to read and understand almost anything by knowing and mastering the alphabet.

I will divide the alphabet in two groups. **Vowels** and **Consonants.**

Spanish language consists of five vowels.

A (a) - *Close to the "A" sound in Apple.*

Amigo – Friend   Amor – Love

E (e) - *Close to the "E" sound in Get.*

Español – Spanish   Estudiante - Student

I (i) - *Close to "ee" sound in Bee or the "i" sound in India.*

Iglesia – Church   Idea – Idea

O (o) - *Close to "oh" sound in Off.*

Ojo – Eye
Oro - Gold

U (u) - *Close to the "oo" sound in food or the "u" sound in Put.*
Uva – Grape
Universo - Universe

Special Case – Caso especial
Y (y griega) - *It sounds like the vowel "i" when it is alone or at the end of a word.*
Y – And
Rey – King

Spanish language consists of twenty-two consonants.
B (be) - *It sounds like in English.*
Bonito – Beautiful
Bueno - Good

*C (ce) - *It sounds like in English.*
Cereal – Cereal
Cerveza - Beer
Check the pronunciation chart for full combinations with all the vowels.

Ch (ce hache) - *It sounds like in English.*
Chocolate – Chocolate   Chorizo – Sausage

Check the pronunciation chart for full combinations with all the vowels with the consonant C.

D (de) - *It sounds like in English.*
Dedo – Finger

Deuda - debt

F (efe) - *It sounds like in English.*
Feo – Ugly
Fuerte - Strong

*G (ge) - *It sounds like in English.*
Gato – Cat
Grande – Big
Check the pronunciation chart for full combinations with all the vowels.

*H (hache) - *It does not sound at all, it is always mute.*
Hotel – Hotel
Hoy - Today
However, in words with foreign spelling and no Spanish equivalent, it sounds like in English: Hawái, Hollywood, hámster, hip-hop, etc.

*J (jota) - *It sounds like the English "h".*
Jabón – Soap
Japón - Japan
It NEVER sounds like the English J.

*K (ka) - *It sounds like in English.*
Kilo – Kilo Kilómetro – Kilometer
You will only find this sound in words coming from Kilo (Latin origin) and some foreign words (kárate – Karate).

L (ele) - *It sounds like in English.*
Lobo – Wolf
Luna - Moon

Ll (elle o doble l) - *It sounds like the English "J" everywhere you find it.*
Llave – Key
Lluvia - Rain
You might not find it anymore in the alphabet in some countries, however, all the words and function are still live and working for this letter.

M (eme) - *It sounds like in English.*
Mano – Hand
Maravilloso – Wonderful

N (ene) - *It sounds like in English.*
Nada – Nothing
Nido – Nest

Ñ (eñe) - *It sounds much like the ni combination in **onion** or the ny combination in **canyon**.*
Araña – Spider
Puño – Fist

P (pe) - *It sounds like in English.*
Pelota – Ball
Pato - Duck

Q (cu) - *It sounds like "k" in English.*
Queso – Chees
Quijada - Jaw

*Always followed by the letter **u**.*

*R (ere) - *It sounds different than in English.*
Caro – Expensive
Ca*rr*o – Car
Rey – King
Rosa – Flower

Pay close attention to this letter, since it could be a challenge for the English speaker.
It is pronounced strong at the beginning of words, but soft in the middle of words. You will also find it doubled, which has a very strong sound.
Check the pronunciation chart for full combinations with all the vowels.

S (ese) - *It sounds like in English.*
Sapo – Frog
Sopa – Soup

T (te)- *It sounds like in English.*
Tomate – Tomato
Tela – Cloth

V (ve) - *It sounds like in English.*
Vino – Wine
Vaso - Glass

W (doble ve o doble u) - *It sounds like in English.*
Whisky - Web
Only found in foreign words.

X (equis) - *It sounds like in English.*

Xenofobia – Xenophobia

Examen – Exam

There are only few words that starts with "X" you will mostly find it in the middle of words.

Pronunciation can be tricky sometimes when at the beginning of a word, it can sound like "s" or "ks" depending on the country. When it is in the middle of word, it always sound like in English.

Special attention:

México   Oaxaca

It sounds like "j" in Spanish or the English "h".

Y (y griega) - *It sounds like "j" in English when it is a consonant.*

Ayer – Yesterday

Yo – I

There are not many words starting with "y", you will mostly find it in the middle of words.

Remember, when it is alone or at the end, it functions as the vowel "i" in Spanish.

Z (zeta) - *It sounds like "s" in English.*

Zapato – Shoe

Zorro - Fox

In many part of Spain it can sound like the "th" in thin, but in all Latin American countries, it sounds like "s".

Pronunciation Chart

Spanish language is formed by combining consonants with vowels, thus giving you a very easy way to learn how to read and differentiate the sounds.

It is very important for you to fully master the chart below so you can read anything in Spanish. By mastering this chart, you will have the ability to pronounce almost like a native Spanish speaker, read in Spanish, recognize the sounds and even take dictation into Spanish.

It does not matter if you do not understand the meaning just yet, we will guide you gradually.

Remember, the sounds in the charts will be the same all over, so you just have to learn it once and you are ready to master Spanish pronunciation.

Ba	Bañera	Bathtub
Be	Bebida	Drink
Bi	Bien	Good / Well
Bo	Boca	Mouth
Bu	Burro	Donkey
Bla	Blanco	White
Ble	Posible	Possible
Bli	Neblina	Fog
Blo	Diablo	Devil
Blu	Blusa	Blouse
Bra	Palabra	Word
Bre	Hombre	Man
Bri	Abril	April

| Bro | Libro | Book |
| Bru | Bruto | Dumb |

Ca	Cama	Bed
*Que	Queso	Cheese
*Qui	Quien	Who
Co	Como	How
Cu	Cuando	When

To complete the five sounds in Spanish the "Qu" is needed, thus giving the correct sound for the full combination.

| *Ce | Cena | Diner |
| *Ci | Cielo | Sky |

Pay close attention to the pronunciation of these two and you will understand it better.

Cla	Clan	Clan
Cle	Bicicleta	Bicycle
Cli	Clínica	Clinic
Clo	Ciclo	Cycle
Clu	Recluta	Recruit

Cra	Cráneo	Skull
Cre	Crédito	Credit
Cri	Crisis	Crisis
Cro	Cromosoma	Chromosome
Cru	Crucero	Cruise

Da	Dama	Lady
De	Dedo	Finger
Di	Día	Day
Do	Domingo	Sunday

Teach Yourself Spanish Level One

Du	Ducha	Shower

No words with Dla combination.

Dra	Dragón	Dragon
Dre	Madre	Mother
Dri	Padrino	Godfather
Dro	Ladrón	Thief
Dru	Madrugada	Dawn
Fa	Famoso	Famous
Fe	Fe	Faith
Fi	Fiebre	Fever
Fo	Fósforos	Matches
Fu	Fuego	Fire
Fla	Flauta	Flute
Fle	Flexible	Flexible
Fli	Conflicto	Conflict
Flo	Flores	Flowers
Flu	Fluido s	Fluids / Liquids
Fra	Frágil	Fragile
Fre	Fresco	Fresh
Fri	Frío	Cold
Fro	Frontera	Frontier
Fru	Fruta	Fruit
Ga	Galleta	Cookie
*Gue	Guerra	War
*Gui	Seguimiento	Follow up
Go	Gota	Drop
Gu	Gusto	Taste

Dr. Yeral E. Ogando

To complete the five sounds in Spanish the "U" is needed, thus giving the correct sound for the full combination.

*Ge	General	General
*Gi	Gigante	Giant

Pay close attention to the pronunciation of these two and you will understand it better.

Gla	Reglas	Rules
Gle	Iglesia	Church
Gli	Negligencia	Negligence
Glo	Siglo	Century
Glu	Glucosa	Glucose
Gra	Gracia	Grace
Gre	Grecia	Greece
Gri	Gripe	Flu
Gro	Milagro	Miracle
Gru	Grupo	Group
Ha	Habitación	Room
He	Helado	Ice Cream
Hi	Hielo	Ice
Ho	Hombro	Shoulder
Hu	Humano	Human

Remember, H is always silent and it only has the combination with the vowels.

Ja	Jamás	Never
Je	Jefe	Boss / Chief
Ji	Jirafa	Giraffe

| Jo | Joven | Young |
| Ju | Juego | Game |

| *Ki | Kilo - Kilo | |

Remember, there are only Latin words with Ki and foreign words with K. Review the "C" section for pronunciation.

La	Labios	Lips
Le	Lengua	Tongue
Li	Libro	Book
Lo	Loco	Crazy
Lu	Luz	Light

Lla	Llave	Key
Lle	Lleno	Full
Lli	Allí	There
Llo	Pollo	Chicken
LLu	Lluvia	Rain

Remember, it is pronounced just like the English J.

Ma	Magia	Magic
Me	Memoria	Memory
Mi	Miembro	Member
Mo	Moderno	Modern
Mu	Música	Music

Na	Nadie	No body
Ne	Negro	Black
Ni	Niño	Boy
No	Noche	Night
Nu	Nunca	Never

Ña	Piña	Pineapple
Ñe	Muñeca	Doll / Wrist
Ñi	Albañil	Builder
Ño	Año	Year
Ñu	Ñu	Gnu (Wildebeest)

Remember, it is hard to find words with "Ñu" in Spanish.

Pa	Padre	Father
Pe	Perro	Dog
Pi	Pierna	Leg
Po	Pobre	Poor
Pu	Puerta	Door

Pla	Placer	Pleasure
Ple	Empleo	Job / Employment
Pli	Disciplina	Discipline
Plo	Ejemplo	Example
Plu	Plural	Plural

Pra	Compra	Purchase
Pre	Pregunta	Question
Pri	Primero	First
Pro	Problema	Problem
Pru	Prueba	Test

Que	Pequeño	Small
Qui	Químico	Chemical / Chemist

These are the only sounds and combinations with the letter "Q" in Spanish.

Ra	Ratón	Mouse
Re	Reacción	Reaction
Ri	Ridículo	Ridiculous
Ro	Roca	Rock
Ru	Rudo	Rude

Sa	Sábado	Saturday
Se	Serio	Serious
Si	Siempre	Always
So	Sol	Sun
Su	Suerte	Luck

Ta	Talento	Talent
Te	Tema	Subject
Ti	Tiempo	Time
To	Todo	Everything
Tu	Turismo	Tourism

*Tla	Atlas	Atlas
Tle	Atleta	Athlete
Tli	Postliminio	Postliminium
Tlo	Decatlón	Decathlon

In Spanish there are a few words with the "TL" combination and these few words are taken from another language or foreign words.

Tra	Trabajo	Work / Job
Tre	Desastre	Disaster
Tri	Triste	Sad
Tro	Tropa	Troop
Tru	Truco	Trick

*Va	Vaca	Cow
Ve	Vena	Vein
Vi	Viaje	Trip
Vo	Vocabulario	Vocabulary
Vu	Vuelo	Flight

Remember, there are no words with "VL and VR" combination. Make sure to check "Bl and Br" combination. You might find it in a foreign name, such as Vladimir (Russian name).

Ya	Yate	Yacht
Ye	Yeso	Plaster
Yi	Ensayista	Essayist
Yo	Yodo	Iodine
Yu	Yuca	Cassava

Remember, there are just a few words with "Y" combination. It works as a consonant when it is between vowels and at the beginning of words.

*Za	Zapato	Shoe
Zo	Brazo	Arm
Zu	Azúcar	Sugar

There are very few words with the "Z" combination; however, you need to pay special attention to these words when writing, because of the spelling, when speaking it sounds just as "s", the tricky part is the spelling for writing.

Pepe y su Camión – Pepe and his truck

Soy Pepe vivo en Estados Unidos, estoy casado

y tengo un camión, en el monto un montón de cosas, pero siempre lo hago en orden alfabético, voy por la ciudad buscando cada cosa de la *A* a la *Z*.

Meto a un *a*migo lleno de *a*mor, a un *bo*nito *bu*rro *bru*to con la *bo*ca *bla*nca, una *ca*ja de *ce*rveza y otra *ca*ja de *ce*real para la *ce*na de la *cla*se que va en el *cru*cero.

Luego monto un *cho*rizo de *cho*colate, una *da*ma *dra*gón *de di*ez *de*dos que se *du*cha el *dí*a *do*mingo, a un *e*studiante de *e*spañol y a una *fu*erte y *fe*a *fo*ca que es *fa*mosa por prender *fu*ego a las *flo*res con los *fó*sforos y crear con*fli*ctos lanzando *fru*tas.

Al rato voy por un *ga*to *gra*nde llamado *Ge*neral al que le *gu*stan las *ga*lletas con *go*tas *gi*gantes de *glu*cosa y pasé por la *ha*bitación del *ho*tel a buscar el *he*lado que estaba en el *hi*elo y un *i*cono que estaba en una *i*glesia, también recogí a la *ji*rafa del *jo*ven *je*fe que no *ju*ega *ja*más.

Un *ki*lómetro después busco un *ki*lo de *ki*wis, a *la luz* de *la lu*na a un *lo*co *lo*bo de *le*ngua *la*rga y bajo la *llu*via hay un po*llo* que está a*llí* con la *lla*ve.

*Mo*nto a un *mú*sico *mo*derno que tiene *ma*nos *ma*ravillosas y hace *ma*gia de *no*che a un *ni*ño *ne*gro que *nu*nca *na*da, también un *ñu* que come *ña*me y un *o*so con *o*jos color *o*ro.

*Pri*mero pa*só por* un *po*bre *pa*to con *pa*ta de *pa*lo que juega *pe*lota con un *pe*rro lleno de *pla*ga y después por *qui*nce *que*sos.

Debo montar el ca*ro* ca*rro* color *ro*sa que pertenece al *re*y y por *ser sá*bado tengo que buscar a un *se*rio *sa*po con *su*erte que *si*empre *to*ma el *so*l. *To*do el *ti*empo busco *te*la color *to*mate y una *u*rna color *uv*a.

Hago un *vi*aje para buscar una *va*ca que toma *va*sos de *vi*no y un *wh*isky que promocionan en la *we*b y después yo recojo a un *yu*goslavo que come *yu*ca y usa un *ye*so. Por último busco a mi amigo que es un *zo*rro que usa *za*patos.

Después de hacer 27 viajes y pasar recogiendo tantas cosas de la *A* a la *Z*, quedo *ex*hausto y debo descansar para al otro día volver a comenzar.

Word List – Listado de palabras

Su camión – His truck. (8)

La ciudad – The city. (3)

Lleno de amor – Full of love.

Una caja de cerveza - A box of beer. (3) (8)

La clase – The class.

Diez – Ten.

Foca – Seal.

Prender fuego – Light on fire.

Con los fósforos – With the matches.

Crear conflictos – Creates conflicts.

Lanzando frutas – Throwing Fruits away. (7)

Al rato voy – Then I go.

Le gustan – He likes. (7)

Y pasé – And I passed. (11)

Buscar – Search / Find.

Que estaba en el hielo – That was in the ice. (13)

Un icono – An Icone.

También recogí – I picked up too.

Después – After / Later.

Busco un kilo de kiwis – A kilo of kiwis.

Larga – Long.

Bajo la lluvia – Under the rain.

Hay un pollo – There is a chicken. (☑ 6)

Que tiene – That has.

Y hace – And does (makes).

Que come ñame – That eats yam.

Un oso con ojos color oro – A bear with Golden eyes.

Pato con pata de palo – A duck with wooden foot.

Que juega – Who plays.

Lleno de plaga – Full of pest.

Por quince quesos – For fifteen cheeses.

Que pertenece al rey – That belongs to the King.

Por ser – For being.

Una urna color uva – An urn of grapes color.

Hago un viaje – I make a trip.

Que promocionan en la web – Which they promote on the web.

Yo recojo a un yugoslavo – I pick up a Yugoslavian.

Que come yuca y usa un yeso – Who eats cassava and wears a cast.

Por último – Last / Finally.

Quedo exhausto – I am exhausted.

Y debo descansar – And I must rest.

Para al otro día – For the next day.

Volver a comenzar – To start again.

A Little bit more – Un poco más

Greetings and Introductions – Saludos y presentaciones.

Hola – Hello / Hi.

Buenos días – Good morning.

Buenas tardes – Good afternoon.

Buenas noches - Good Evening (Good night when leaving)

¿Aló? - Hello? This is a common way of answering the phone in many Spanish-speaking countries.

Adiós - Bye. / Goodbye.

Hasta luego - See you later.

Hasta pronto - See you soon.

Hasta mañana - See you tomorrow.

¿Cómo está Usted? – How are you? (Formal, Polite, respect).

¿Cómo estás? – How are you? (Informal, with a friend of acquaintance).

¿Cómo están? - How are you? (Plural).

Bien – Well / Fine.

Mal – Bad.

Más o menos – More or less.

No muy bien – Not so good.

Muy bien – Very well.

¿De dónde eres? - Where are you from?

Soy de Francia – I am from France.

Bienvenidos – Welcome.

¿Cómo te llamas? - What's your name?

Me llamo Pedro - My name is Pedro.

Mi nombre es Pedro – My name is Pedro.

¿Y usted? – And you? (Formal, polite)

¿Y tú? – And you? (Informal with friends and acquaintance).

Mucho gusto - Nice to meet you.

Encantado de conocerle – Nice to meet you.

Igualmente – Likewise.

Phrases and Expressions – Frases y expresiones.

Tengo hambre - I'm hungry

Tengo sed - I'm thirsty

¿Puedo ver al menú, por favor? - May I have a menu, please?

¿Qué me aconseja? - What do you recommend?

Quisiera... - I'd like...

¿Puede darme...? - May I have some...?

¿Podría darme más...? - Can I have some more...?

¿Tiene usted fruta fresca? - Do you have fresh fruit?

Nada más, gracias. - Nothing more, thank you.

¿Dónde está el baño? - Where is the bathroom?

¿Dónde está el supermercado? - Where is the supermarket?

Quisiéramos sentarnos en la sección de no fumadores, por favor. - We would like to sit in the non-smoking section please.

Mesero / Mesera - Waiter / Waitress

Quisiera desayunar. - I would like some breakfast.

Estoy a dieta. - I'm on a diet.

Exercises - Ejercicios

1- How many letters does the Spanish alphabet have?_____

2- How does LL sound when spoken?

_____

3- How does Z sound when spoken?

_____

4- Introduce yourself using one sentence.

_____

5- Greet a friend whose name is David using one

sentence._____

6- Write three words with "Ch".

_____

7- Write two words with "Rr"

_____

Reading Comprehension:

¿Dónde vive Pepe? – Where does Pepe live?

¿Cuántos kilos de kiwi buscó? – How many pounds of Kiwi he searched?

¿De qué color es la urna? – What color is the urn?

Knowledge Base
Argentine Republic - República Argentina
Motto: En unión y libertad - In Unity and Freedom.
Capital and largest city - Buenos Aires
Recognized regional languages
Guaraní, Qom, Mocoví and Wichi, in Chaco.

De facto languages - Spanish.
Population - 2015 estimate - 43,417,000.
Currency - Peso ($) (ARS)
Calling code - +54

Though not declared official de jure, the Spanish language is the only one used in the wording of laws, decrees, resolutions, official documents and public acts.

The almost-unparalleled increase in prosperity led to Argentina becoming the seventh wealthiest developed nation in the world by the early 20th century.

Bible Verse - Versículo Bíblico

El que no ama, no ha conocido a Dios; porque Dios es amor. 1 Juan 4:8

Lesson 2

Mis Amigos – My friends

Somos cinco amigos y nosotros hacemos muchas cosas juntos. *Alquilamos* una habitación por cuarenta y dos dólares y allí vivimos todos. Somos dos chicos y tres chicas. Mi nombre es Carlos, mi amigo es José, las chicas son María, Ana y Doris.

Los propietarios son una pareja de ancianos de setenta y nueve y noventa *y* cuatro años de edad, ellos *cobran* la renta, *necesitan* dinero para pagar un préstamo de cien dólares.

José tiene diez y siete años, *estudia* medicina, él quiere ser doctor. *También habla* español pero no *canta ni tampoco ayuda* a los niños.

Doris tiene quince años, ella quiere ser profesora y *ayuda* a doce niños a hacer sus tareas, ella *busca* las respuestas a las preguntas que les hacen en la escuela. Ella no *habla* español *pero* sí inglés.

María y Ana son hermanas, María tiene veintiún años y Ana veintitrés y ellas no *estudian ni tampoco hablan* español. Ellas *trabajan* en un laboratorio y también *analizan* los resultados. Ellas *cuentan* que a veces a los pacientes les cuesta aceptar la verdad.

Yo tengo veinte años, *estudio* música, sé cantar muy bien y también sé hablar español. María cumple años hoy. Ana y yo salimos a comprar la comida y el pastel al salir del trabajo. Ella me *manda* un mensaje de texto para encontrarnos en el supermercado. Yo salgo de la habitación, pero antes *borro* el texto para que María no lo vea y que su fiesta sea una sorpresa.

Al llegar a la habitación nosotros *hablamos* con José y con Doris acerca de la fiesta, ellos están contentos. Cuando María llega todos salimos a cantar cumple años feliz.

Word List – Listado de palabras

Mis Amigos - My friends

Somos cinco amigos - We are five friends (5)

Nosotros hacemos - We do / Make (4)
Muchas cosas juntos - Many things together
Alquilamos una habitación- We rent a room

Allí vivimos todos - All of us live there (4)
Somos dos chicos y tres chicas. - We are two boy and three girls.
Mi amigo es José - My Friend Jose.

Las chicas - The girls. (3)
Los propietarios - The landlords.
Una pareja de ancianos - An elderly couple.
Ellos cobran la renta - They charge (collect) the rent.
Necesitan dinero - They need money.
Para pagar un préstamo - To pay a loan.
Él quiere ser doctor - He wants to be a doctor.
Ella quiere ser profesora - She wants to be a teacher.
Sus tareas - Their home-works.
Las respuestas a las preguntas - The answers to the

questions.

Que les hacen en la escuela - They do (make) at school.

Son hermanas - They are sisters.

Ellas no estudian ni tampoco hablan español - They don't study and they don't speak Spanish either.

Ellas trabajan en un laboratorio - They work in a lab.

También analizan los resultados - They analyze the results as well.

Ellas cuentan que a veces - They say that sometimes.

A los pacientes les cuesta aceptar la verdad - Patients find it hard to accept the truth.

María cumple años hoy - Is Maria's birthday today.

Ella me manda un mensaje de texto - She sends me a text message.

Para encontrarnos en el supermercado - To meet us at the supermarket.

Yo salgo de la habitación - I get out of the bedroom.

Pero antes borro el texto - But I delete the text before.

Para que María no lo vea - So Maria does not see it.

Que su fiesta sea una sorpresa - So his party be a surprise.

Al llegar a la habitación - Upon arriving to the bedroom.

Acerca de la fiesta - about the party.

Ellos están contentos - They are happy.

Cuando María llega - When Maria arrives.

Todos salimos - We all go out.

A cantar cumpleaños feliz - To sing Happy Birthday.

✍ Grammar Explanations – Notas gramaticales

🔒 Personal Pronouns – Pronombres personales.

Yo	I
Tú	You
Usted	You (Polite form)
Él	He
Ella	She
Nosotros	We
Ustedes	You
Ellos (as)	They

Remarks:

Tú is used among friends, coworkers, relatives, or when addressing a child.

Usted is used as a polite form when speaking to an Elder person, higher Rank, someone you meet for the first time or showing respect.

Nosotros is the masculine form for *We* and *Nosotras* is the feminine form. Whenever there are two or more person together and there is at least a man, Spanish speaking people refer to the group as *Nosotros* – *We* masculine form.

Ellos is the masculine form for *They* and *Ellas* is the feminine form. Whenever there are two or more person together and there is at least a man, Spanish speaking people refer to the group as *Ellos* – *They* masculine form.

*You will not see the "**Vosotros**" form in this book. Since it is mostly used in Spain.*

Simple Present – Presente simple.

In Spanish there are three groups of verbs, you will know when a verb is in its infinitive form (non-conjugated or dictionary form) by their ending "***Ar – Er – Ir.***"

First Group of verb (Ar).

To conjugate a verb in Spanish you just need to drop the ending or infinitive (Ar – Er – Ir) and add the corresponding conjugation, as you will see below.

Hablar - Speak / Talk

Yo	habl*o*
Tú	habl*as*
Usted	habl*a*
Él	habl*a*
Ella	habl*a*
Nosotros	habl*amos*
Ustedes	habl*an*
Ellos (as)	habl*an*

Remarks:

As you can see, you drop the "***Ar***" from Habl*ar* and it leaves you with the root ***habl,*** then you add the corresponding ending.

*First person (Yo – I) always ends in **O**.*
*Yo Habl**o** Español – I speak Spanish.*
*Second person (Tú – You) always ends in **AS**.*
*Tú habl**as** Italiano – You speak Italian.*
Third person (Usted – You / Él – He and Ella –

She) always have the same ending A.

Usted habla Español – You speak Spanish (polite).
Él habla Inglés – He speaks English.
Ella habla Alemán – She speaks German.
First person plural (Nosotros – We) always ends in
AMOS.

Nosotros hablamos Francés – We speak French.
Second person of the plural (Ustedes – You / Ellos (as) – They) always ends in **AN**.

Ustedes hablan Ruso – You speak Russian.
Ellos hablan Japonés – They speak Japanese.

Most of the verbs from the first group (AR) are regular and they follow the same pattern.

Estudiar – Study

Yo	estudi**o**
Tú	estudi**as**
Usted / Él / Ella	estudi**a**
Nosotros	estudi**amos**
Ustedes / Ellos (as)	estudi**an**

Yo estudio Ingles – I study English
Tú estudias Español – You study Spanish

Cantar – Sing

Yo	cant**o**
Tú	cant**as**
Usted / Él / Ella	cant**a**
Nosotros	cant**amos**
Ustedes / Ellos (as)	cant**an**

Nosotros cantamos música americana – We sing American music
Ellos cantan Bachata - They sing Bachata

You are now ready to conjugate any regular verb from the first group and use it in simple sentences with the large vocabulary you already have. Before giving you a list of verbs for your practice, let us first learn how to ask and answer in Spanish.

How to ask and answer questions – Como preguntar y responder.

You just place the personal pronoun after the conjugation of the verb to ask questions.

*¿Habl*a* Usted Español?* – Do you speak Spanish?

*Si, habl*o* Español* – Yes, I speak Spanish.

*No, no habl*o* Español* – No, I don't speak Spanish.

*¿Cant*as* tú música americana?* – Do you sing american music?

*Si, cant*o* un poco de música americana* – Yes, I sing a little bit of american music.

*No, no cant*o* bien música americana* – No, I do not sing well american music.

*We use question marks at the beginning and at the end in Spanish. There is an opening and a closing mark. Pay close attention.

* In Spanish is not an obligation to use personal pronouns when speaking, because with the ending of the verb it is well understood whom you are referring to. Pay close attention to this.

*¿Cant*as* música americana?* – Do you sing american music?

As you can see the conjugation or ending of the verb **AS** tells you that you are referring to the personal pronoun *Tú.*

Short cut to quick learning Spanish.
Y – And: We use it to join two affirmative sentences.

También – Too: We use it at the end of two affirmative sentences. But also in the middle or beginning of words, when the first part of the sentence is understood. You will learn the different uses as you progress in your learning experience.

Pero – But: We use it to join an affirmative and a negative sentence and vice versa.

Yo habl*o* Español *y* habl*o* Inglés *también.* – I speak Spanish and I speak English too.
Yo no hablo Español
Yo habl*o* Ingles, *pero* no habl*o* Español. – I speak English, but I do not speak Spanish.
Yo no hablo Español, pero hablo Inglés. – I don't speak Spanish, but I speak English.

Ni - Tampoco – Either: We use it at the end of two negative sentences. Pay close attention, the word for Either is Tampoco, however, to unite the sentence Spanish speakers use the particle "Ni".
Yo no habl*o* Español *ni* hablo Inglés *tampoco.* – I don't speak Spanish and I don't speak English either.

Verb list from "Ar" Group – Lista de verbos del grupo "Ar"
Here you have a list of verbs from the first Group

41

to conjugate them and use them in sentences (ask and answers, positive and negative).

Aceptar la verdad – Accept the truth
Alquilar una habitación – Rent a room
Analizar el resultado – Analyze the result
Ayudar a los niños – Help the children
Borrar el texto – Delete the text
Buscar la respuesta – Search for the answer
Cobrar la renta – Collect the rent
Comprar la comida – Buy the food
Necesitar dinero – Need money
Pagar el préstamo – Pay the loan

A little bit more – Un poco más

Números cardinales - Cardinal Numbers

1 – uno	2 - dos
3 – tres	4 - cuatro
5 – cinco	6 - seis
7 – siete	8 - ocho
9 – nueve	10 - diez
11 – once	12 - doce
13 – trece	14 - catorce
15 – quince	16 - dieciséis
17 – diecisiete	18 - dieciocho
19 – diecinueve	20 - **veinte**
21 – veintiuno	22 - veintidós
23 – veintitrés	30 - **treinta**
40 – cuarenta	50 - cincuenta
60 – sesenta	70 - setenta
80 – ochenta	90 - noventa
*100 – cien	

Remarks:
The most important part is to learn the numbers from *1 - 20*. As you can see, after twenty, you just need to add the numbers from *1-9*. Use the conjunction *Y – And* to join them.

Treinta y uno	– 31	Treinta y dos	- 32
Cuarenta y uno	– 41	Cuarenta y dos	- 42

101 - ciento uno
125 - ciento veinticinco
200 - doscientos
300 - trescientos
400 - cuatrocientos
500 - quinientos
600 - seiscientos
700 - setecientos
800 - ochocientos
900 - novecientos
1000 - mil
1.000.000 - un millón
10.000.000 - diez millones

Cien and Ciento - 100
We use *Cien* when we refer to the exact number (100) or when we use it with substantives.
Cien = 100
Cien libros – 100 books
Cien mujeres - 100 women
It does not matter if it is masculine or feminine.
We use *Ciento* when we refer to compound numbers by hundred plus other numbers (101, 102,

etc.)
   101 = Ciento uno
   164 = ciento sesenta y cuatro
   190 = ciento noventa

Exercises – Ejercicios
1.   When is a verb in its infinitive form?

_____

2.   Conjugate the verb "Amar".

_____

3.   Name singular personal pronouns.

_____

4.   Name plural personal pronouns.

_____

5.   Fill the blank spaces with también or tampoco:

Yo hablo español y _____ hablo inglés.

El no

canta música americana ni _____ música
española. (Spanish music)
   6.   Write down the following numbers:

123_____

538_____

416_____

  7. Use the verb "cantar "in the following sentences:

Yo _____ música Country.

Ella _____ muy bien.

Nosotros _____ en navidad. (Christmas)

Ustedes _____ música Americana.

  8. Use the verb "caminar" in the following sentences:

Él _____ hasta su casa. (to his house)

Ellos _____ lentamente. (slowly)

Tú _____ todos los días. (everydays)

Reading Comprehension:

  ¿Cuántos amigos son? – How many friends are they?

¿Cuántos años tienen nuestros propietarios? – How old are the landlords?

¿Quién cumple años? – Whose birthday is it?

Knowledge Base
Plurinational State of Bolivia
Estado Plurinacional de Bolivia
Motto: La unión es la fuerza - Unity is Strength.
Capital - Sucre
Largest city - Santa Cruz de la Sierra
Official languages
Spanish, Quechua, Aymara, Guarani and 33 other native languages
Demonym - Bolivian
Government - Unitary presidential constitutional republic
President - Evo Morales
Vice President - Álvaro García Linera
Population - 2015 estimate - 11,410,651
Currency - Boliviano (BOB)
Calling code - +591
While Sucre is the constitutional capital, La Paz is the seat of the government..

Bible Verse - Versículo Bíblico
No seas vencido de lo malo, sino vence con el bien el mal. **Romanos 12:21**

Lesson 3 🔒

Me voy de tiendas – I go shopping

Mi nombre es Brenda, amo *las* compras. Hoy después de tener una conversación con *una amiga* hice *una* solicitud en mi trabajo para salir temprano. No hay discusión cuando comienzo a hablar, le di a mi jefe *una buena* explicación, ella dice que sí puedo ir que no hay problema, pero que no se haga costumbre ya que en *la oficina* hay mucha actividad. Digo adiós cierro *la puerta* y me voy.

Qué felicidad, me monto en *el carro*, cuelgo *el abrigo*, prendo *la radio*, saco *el mapa*, consigo *la tienda* a la que voy y arranco. Llego *al estacionamiento* y *los atletas* están allí, escucho la voz que dice por *el parlante* que *los carros* deben salir y estacionar a diez cuadras de allí. Me monto en *el carro* y diez cuadras después logro estacionar frente al consultorio de un psiquiatra.

Me bajo del carro con mí vestido de trabajo y *los zapatos* de tacón, soy la reina de las compras en la ciudad y *estoy* a diez cuadras, no son nada para mí. Un señor me toca *la mano* y descubro que es *el profesor* de mi hermano y me dice que el martes *el niño* no llevó ni *los libros* ni su lápiz. Hago un análisis y recuerdo que *el lápiz* y *los libros* del niño están sobre *la mesa* de *la televisión* al lado de *la lámpara*.

Sólo camino dos **cuadras** y **comienza** a llover, el día tiene **un clima** frío, **el planeta está** loco, **estamos** en agosto. Comienzo a toser, el tórax me duele y **la cabeza** también. No me importa, camino tres cuadras más, me siento caliente y un poco mareada.

Soy la reina de **las compras** en **la ciudad**, pero hoy no es el día para comprar, regreso al carro, me monto y me dirijo a casa. No pude comprar, al llegar debo calentar **la comida**, comer, tomarme **una aspirina** e irme a la cama con **el gato**. Mañana será otro día, convenceré a mi jefe y me iré a comprar.

Word List – Listado de palabras

Me voy de tiendas – I go shopping. (3)
Amo las compras – I love shopping.
Después de tener una conversación – After having a conversation.
Hice una solicitud en mi trabajo – I made a request at my work.
Para salir temprano – To get out earlier.
No hay discusión – There is no discussion.
Cuando comienzo a hablar – When I start to speak.
Le di a mi jefe una buena explicación – I gave by boss a good explanation.
Ella dice que sí puedo ir – She says that I can go.
Pero que no se haga costumbre – But that it does not become a habit.
Ya que en la oficina – Because at the office.
Hay mucha actividad – There are many activities (busy – lots of work).
Digo adiós – I say goodbye. (3)

Y me voy. – And I leave.

Qué felicidad – What a happiness.

Prendo la radio – I turn on the radio.

Saco el mapa – Pull out the map.

Consigo la tienda - I locate the store.

A la que voy – Which I am going.

Y arranco. – And I start.

Por el parlante - Through the speaker.

Que los carros deben salir – That cars must go out.

A diez cuadras de allí – Ten blocks away from there.

Después logro estacionar - Later I manage to park.

Frente al consultorio de un psiquiatra – In front of a psychiatrist office.

Me bajo del carro – I get off the car.

Con mí vestido de trabajo – With my work dress.

Y los zapatos de tacón – And high heeled shoes.

Soy la reina de las compras – I am the queen of shopping.

En la ciudad - In the city.

No son nada para mí – They are nothing for me (no challenge).

Un señor me toca la mano – A man touches my hand.

El profesor de mi hermano – My brother's teacher.

No llevó ni los libros ni su lápiz – He did not take books nor pencils.

Están sobre la mesa de la televisión – They are on the tv table.

Al lado de la lámpara – Next to the lamp.

El día tiene un clima frío – The weather is cold today.

Está loco – It is crazy.

No me importa - It doesn't matter (I don't care).

Me siento caliente y un poco mareada. – I feel warm and a little dizzy.

Pero hoy no es el día – But today is not the day.

Y me dirijo a casa – And I head home.

No pude comprar – I could not shop. (✏️ 3)

Tomarme una aspirina - Take an aspirin.

*E irme a la cama con el gato – And go to bed with the cat. *(Y means and, the conjuction, but when the next word starts with an "I" in Spanish, we change the "I" by "E – and" to have a better sound).*

Mañana será otro día – Tomorrow will be another day. (✏️ 3)

Convenceré a mi jefe – I will convince my boss.

Me iré a comprar. – I will go shopping.

✏️ Grammar Explanations – Notas gramaticales

🔒 Gender of Nouns – Genero de los nombres o sustantivos.

A noun is a word used to denote a person, place, thing, or idea. In Spanish, all nouns are either masculine or feminine. In Spanish all living creatures are easy to identify the gender male or female. Every noun in Spanish has a specific article that denotes the gender of the word. They can be definite or indefinite and have four forms:

Masculine Singular	Masculine Plural
El niñ*o* – The boy	*Los* niñ*os* – The boys
El libr*o* – The book	*Los* libr*os* – The books
El gat*o* – The cat	*Los* gat*os* – The cats

Feminine Singular	Feminine Plural
La niñ*a* – The girl	*Las* niñ*as* – The girls
La cas*a* – The house	*Las* cas*as* – The houses
La cam*a* – The bed	*Las* cam*as* – The beds

General rules for identifying the gender.

When speaking about living creatures every word that ends in *O* is masculine and every word that ends in *A* is feminine. Only distinct living creatures fall under this categorization.

Masculine	*Feminine*
El niñ*o* – The boy	*La* niñ*a* – The girl
Los niñ*os* – The boys	*Las* niñ*as* – The girls

Definite Article – Articulo Definido

As you can see by learning the gender of things, you have also learned the definite article *"The"*

Masculine Singular	Masculine Plural
El	Los
Feminine Singular	**Feminine Plural**
La	Las

Pay close attention to the tricky part in Spanish. When determining the gender of an object or thing, do not try to analyze the nature of the object, looking for some inherent masculinity or femininity.

El vestid*o* – The dress

You might think that because it ends in *O*, it should be masculine, but it is not. That is why you need to learn every noun with its article (*El, La*), that way you will know what the gender is. You might ask yourself. Why? Well, because:

You cannot predict the gender of most nouns.

Not every noun that ends in -*o* is masculine, and not every noun that ends in -*a* is feminine.

Many nouns end in letters other than *o* or *a*.

Some nouns referring to professions have the same form for masculine and feminine, the only thing that identify them is the article.

El atleta – The male athlete

La atleta – The female athlete

El psiquiatra – The male psychiatrist

La psiquiatra – The female psychiatrist

Whenever you see nouns that end in – *sión, – ción, – dad, – tud and – umbre*, you will always require the feminine article.

La conversa*ción* – The conversation

La discu*sión* – The discussion

La solici*tud* – The application

La cost*umbre* – The custom

La activi*dad* – The activity

Whenever you see a nouns ending in – *ma*, you need to use the masculine article.

El problema – The problem

A few nouns ending in – Ma are feminine, but the general rule is that they are masculine.

La cama – The bed

Whenever you see a masculine noun ending in a consonant, that noun forms the feminine part by just adding the "*a*" ending.

El señor – The Mr.

La señora – The Mrs.

El doctor – The male doctor

La doctora – The female doctor

You will also find some masculine nouns ending in *A*.

El planeta – The planet

El día – The day

El mapa – The map

El clima – The weather

You will also find some feminine nouns ending in *O*.

La radio – The radio

La mano – The hand

Remember and do not forget, whenever there is a group together, if there is even one that I masculine or male, the gender must always be *Masculine.*

Indefinite Article – Articulo Indefinido

We have seen the four forms of the definite article (El – Los, La – Las), let us now see the four forms for the indefinite article "*A-An*".

Masculine Singular	Masculine Plural
Un carr*o* – A car	*Unos* carr*os* – Some cars
Un libr*o* – A book	*Unos* libr*os* – Some books

Feminine Singular

Una lámpar*a* – A lamp

Una mes*a* – A table

Feminine Plural

Unas lámpar*as* – Some lamps

Unas mes*as* – Some tables

As you can see, it is very easy to use, since you already know the gender of things.

Plural of Nouns – Plural de los nombres.

You might have already noticed from previous

sections that most of the nouns make their plural by adding "*S*" to their form.

Add an S to the nouns that end in vowels

Niño – Boy	Niño*s* – Boys
Libro – Book	Libro*s* – Books
Cama – Bed	Cama*s* – Beds
Zapato – Shoe	Zapato*s* – Shoes

As you can see as long as the noun ends in a vowel, you just need to add *S*, no distinction if it is a masculine or feminine noun.

Remember that if you are using the articles with nouns, they need to match the plural of things as well.

El niñ*o* – The boy	*Los* niñ*os* – The boys
La cam*a* – The bed	*Las* cam*as* – The beds
Un zapat*o* – A shoe	*Unos* zapat*os* – Some shoes
Una mes*a* – A table	*Unas* mes*as* – Some tables

You must always match gender and number (singular and / or plural).

Whenever a noun ends in consonant, you add "*ES*" to make the plural.

Profesor – Teacher	Profesor*es* – Teachers
Rey – King	Rey*es* – Kings
Ciudad – City	Ciudad*es* – Cities

Whenever a noun ends in "*ión*", first drop the accent on the "*o*" and then add "*ES*" to make the plural.

Explicac*ión* – Explanation
Explicacion*es* – Explanations
Conversac*ión* – Conversation
Conversacion*es* – Conversations
Televis*ión* – Television

Television*es* – Televisions

Whenever a noun ends in *Z*, first substitute the *Z* by *C* and then add *"ES"* to make the plural.

Vo*z* – Voice   Vo*ces* – Voices

Lápi*z* – Pencil   Lápi*ces* – Pencils

Whenever you see a noun that ends in "*S*" or "*X*". It does not change. It is the case with most days of the week.

Martes – Tuesday and Tuesdays

Tórax – *Thorax and Thoraxes*

Análisis - *A*nalysis and Analyses

The only thing that could change is if you use these nouns with an article.

El martes – The Tuesday

Los martes – The Tuesdays

Irregular verbs from the first group *"AR".* – *Verbos irregulares del grupo "Ar".*

Calentar la comida – Warm the food

Yo calient*o* la comida – I warm up the food.

Tú calient*as* la comida – You warm up the food.

Usted / *Él* / Ella calient*a* la comida – He warms up the food.

Nosotros calent*amos* la comida – We warm up the food.

Ustedes / *Ellos* (as)   calient*an*   la   comida – They warm up the food.

Cerrar la puerta – Close the door

Yo cierr*o* la puerta – I close the door.

Tú cierr*as* la puerta – You close the door.

Usted / Él / *Ella* cierr*a* la puerta – She closes the

door.

Nosotros cerram*os* la puerta – We close the door.

Ustedes / ***Ellos*** (as)   cierr*an* la puerta – They close the door.

Colgar el abrigo – Hang the coat

Yo cuelg*o* el abrigo – I hang the coat.

Tú cuelg*as* el abrigo – You hang the coat.

Usted / ***Él*** / Ella cuelg*a* el abrigo – He hangs the coat.

Nosotros colg*amos* el abrigo – We hang the coat.

Ustedes / Ellos (as)   cuelg*an* el abrigo – You hang the coat.

Comenzar a hablar – Start to speak

Yo comienzo a hablar – I start to speak.

Tú comienzas a hablar – You start to speak.

Usted / ***Él*** / Ella comienza a hablar – He starts to speak.

Nosotros comenzamos a hablar – We start to speak.

Ustedes / ***Ellos*** (as)   comienzan a hablar – They start to speak.

As you may have seen, the ending stays the same in these verbs, they are irregular because of a slight vowel change in the verb itself.

A little bit more – Un poco más

Días de la semana - Days of the week

Domingo – Sunday

Lunes – Monday

Martes - Tuesday

Teach Yourself Spanish Level One

Miércoles - Wednesday
Jueves - Thursday
Viernes - Friday
Sábado - Saturday
Meses del año - Months of the year
Enero - January
Febrero - February
Marzo - March
Abril - April
Mayo - May
Junio - June
Julio - July
Agosto - August
Septiembre - September
Octubre - October
Noviembre - November
Diciembre - December
Estaciones del año - Seasons of the year.
Primavera - Spring
Verano - Summer
Otoño - Fall
Invierno - Winter

Exercises - Ejercicios
1- Fill in the blanks using la, las, lo, los, el.

_____ niñas llevaron _____ muñeca y

_____ niños

llevaron _____ balón.
2-Fill in the blanks using un, una, unos, unas.

_____ perros persiguien a _____ niña, mientrás

_____ niño les tira _____ palos.

3- Determine if the following words are feminine or masculine.

Agua._____

Cuaderno._____

Silla._____

Sal._____

4- What are the plurals of the following words?

Invierno:_____

Rey:_____

Domingo:_____

Comida_____

Televisión._____

5 Write down the first three days of the week.

_____

6 In what season do we…?

Hacemos muñecos de nieve._____
(snowman)

Vamos a la playa._____
(The leaves fall)

Vemos las ojas caer._____
7- Write down a sentence using: martes, octubre and otoño.

_____

Reading Comprehension:

¿Cuál es mi nombre? – What is my name?
¿Dónde estaciono? – Where do I park?
¿Qué me duele? – Where do I have a pain?

Knowledge Base
Republic of Chile - República de Chile
Motto: Por la razón o la fuerza - By right or might.
Capital and largest city - Santiago
National language – Spanish
Demonym - Chilean
Government - Unitary presidential constitutional republic
President - Michelle Bachelet
Population - 2015 estimate - 18,006,407
Currency - Peso (CLP)
Calling code - +56
Legislature is based in Valparaíso.
Includes Easter Island and Isla Sala y Gómez; does not include 1,250,000 square kilometers of territory claimed in Antarctica.

Bible Verse - Versículo Bíblico

Porque por gracia sois salvos por medio de la fe; y esto no de vosotros, pues es don de Dios. - **Efesios 2:8**

Lesson 4 🔒

Hablando con Mamá – Speaking with Mom.

Andrea: Hola mamá, ¿cómo **estás**?, ¿puedo hablar contigo?

Mamá: Bien, hija. No **tienes** que pedir permiso para hablar, llama cuando **quieras**

Andrea: Te extraño y **siento** necesidad de hablar contigo siempre.

Mamá: Y yo a ti. **Cuéntame** de tus clases de italiano.

Andrea: Ayer insistí en hablar con el director y recibí buenas noticias sobre el curso y que **puedo** venir a estudiar italiano cada día. Esto es muy importante para mí porque dentro de tres semanas **parto** para Italia, y **quiero** saber hablar en público.

Mamá: Esa es una gran noticia. Yo decidí hablar con Pedro sobre el trabajo y ahora voy a vender autos por las tardes. **Discutimos** sobre la situación económica del país y le dije que aunque tengo mucho trabajo en la oficina, **debo** dinero y **tengo** que pagarlo.

Andrea: Qué bueno mamá, tú también **tienes** buenas noticias. ¿**Dime** cómo va tu dieta?.

Mamá: Muy bien, tomo jugo de limón todas las mañanas, luego desayuno con uvas, manzanas, mango y piña. Durante el día me **traen** la comida hasta la oficina, unos días pollo o carne y los otros pescado o langosta, siempre acompañados de arroz.

Además de comer sano, *corro* todos los días y *subo* las escaleras del apartamento diez veces todas las noches, después tomo un baño y *duermo* como un bebé.

Andrea: Qué bueno que te llevan la comida, pues no eres muy buena cocinera, cuando no *rompes* los vasos, le *prendes* fuego a la cocina. Eres la mejor mamá del mundo, pero no una buena cocinera. *Siento* decírtelo, pero *sabes* que *digo* la verdad todo el tiempo.

Mamá: No te preocupes hija, sé que soy mala cocinera y me encanta que digas la verdad todo el tiempo, ya que me siento orgullosa de que *creas* en Dios, *cumplas* sus mandamientos, vayas todos los domingos a la iglesia y le des de comer a los niños hambrientos.

Andrea: Por cierto mamá, conocí a un chico en la iglesia. Terminamos saliendo a ver una película, es una película que iba a ver con mis amigos. Él es todo un caballero, condujo el vehículo hasta la casa y me abrió la puerta del carro.

Mama: Me alegra, pero no *quiero* que descuides tus clases, ¿ya entiendes bien el idioma español? Recuerda que debes *hacer* ejercicios para aprender mejor.

Andrea: No te preocupes mamá, voy a seguir estudiando para aprender bien. Ya sabes que quiero aprender bien el español antes del fin del curso, hasta le escribí un e-mail al profesor de español. Aprendo español en la escuela y quiero hacerlo bien al final del curso, para que me aplaudan al final del discurso.

Mamá: ¿Y qué tal es el profesor de inglés?

Andrea: No *conozco* muy bien al profesor de

inglés. Qué bueno que me enviaste el dinero, ahora voy a poder comprar el libro de inglés y eso es importante ya que debo comprender el inglés muy bien. Mamá *debo* colgar, te amo.

Mamá: Y yo a ti, que Dios te bendiga.

Word List – Listado de palabras

Hablando con Mamá – Speaking with Mom. (14)

¿Puedo hablar contigo? – Can I speak with you?

Bien, hija – Ok, Daughter.

No tienes que - You don't have to.

Pedir permiso – Ask permission.

Llama cuando quieras – Call whenever you want.

Te extraño – I miss you.

Y siento necesidad de hablar – And I feel the need to speak.

Y yo a ti. – And I do to (I miss you too).

Ayer insistí – I insisted yesterday. (11)

Recibí buenas noticias – I received good news.

Cada día – Every day / Each day.

Esto es muy importante – This is important.

Para mí – For me.

Parto para Italia - I leave for Italy.

Esa es una gran noticia. – This is a great news.

Yo decidí – I decided.

Y le dije – And I told him.

Aunque – Even.

Siempre acompañados de arroz – Always accompanied with rice.

Las escaleras del apartamento – The stairs of the

apartment.

Pues no eres muy buena cocinera – Because you are not a good cook.

Eres la mejor mamá del mundo – You are the best Mom in the world.

Siento decírtelo – I am sorry to tell you.

Todo el tiempo – All the time.

Sé que soy mala cocinera – I know I am a bad cook.

Me siento orgullosa – I am proud of you (I feel proud of you). (6)

Cumplas sus mandamientos – Follow His commandments.

Por cierto mamá - By the way Mom.

Conocí a un chico en la iglesia – I met a boy at the church.

Que iba a ver – That he was going to watch.

Él es todo un caballero – He is a real gentleman.

Condujo el vehículo - Drove his car.

Me abrió la puerta del carro. – Opened the car's door. (11)

No quiero que descuides – I do not want you to neglect. (19)

Antes del fin del curso – Before the end of the course.

Hasta le escribí un e-mail - I even emailed him.

¿Y qué tal es el profesor de inglés? – And how about the English teacher?

Qué bueno que me enviaste el dinero – It is good you sent me money.

Mamá debo colgar – Mom, I must go (I must hang up).

Que Dios te bendiga. – God bless you.

Grammar Explanations – Notas gramaticales

Simple Present – Presente simple.

Second Group of verbs (Er). – Verbos del segundo grupo "Er".

To conjugate a verb in Spanish you just need to drop the ending or infinitive (Er) and add the corresponding conjugation, as you will see below.

Comer - Eat

Yo	com*o*
Tú	com*es*
Usted	com*e*
Él	com*e*
Ella	com*e*
Nosotros	com*emos*
Ustedes	com*en*
Ellos (as)	com*en*

Remarks:

As you can see, you just need to drop the "ER" and then add the corresponding ending to conjugate the verbs of the second group.

First person singular "*Yo – I*" always ends in "*O*".

Yo com*o* arroz – I eat rice.

Second person singular "*Tú – You*" always ends in "*ES*".

Tú com*es* carne – You eat meat.

Third person singular "*Usted – You (polite form) / Él – He and Ella – She*" always ends in "*E*".
Usted com*e* pescado – You eat fish.
Él com*e* piña – He eats pineapple.
Ella com*e* pollo – She eats chicken.

First person of plural "*Nosotros – We*" always ends in "*EMOS*".
Nosotros com*emos* langosta – We eat lobster.

Second and third person plural
"*Ustedes – You / Ellos (as) – They*" always ends in "*EN*".
Ustedes com*en* mango – You eat mango.
Ellos com*en* uvas – They eat grapes.
Ellas com*en* manzanas – They eat apples.

As you can see, it is almost the same as with the first group. If you have not noticed, first group ends in "AR" so all the combinations take "A", except for "Yo – I", which will always be "O". Second group ends in "ER" so all the combinations take "E", except for "Yo – I", which will always be "O". See below.

First Group Ar		Second Group Er
Yo	O	O
Tú	AS	ES
Usted / Él / Ella	A	E
Nosotros	AMOS	EMOS
Ustedes / Ellos (as)	AN	EN

Regular verbs from the second Group "ER" – Verbos regulares del segundo grupo "Er".

Aprender español en la escuela – Learn Spanish at school.

Yo *aprendo español en la escuela.* - I learn Spanish at school.

Tú *aprendes español en la escuela.* - You learn Spanish at school.

Usted / Él / **Ella** *aprende español en la escuela.* - She learns Spanish at school.

Nosotros *aprendemos español en la escuela.* - We learn Spanish at school.

Ustedes / **Ellos** (as) *aprenden español en la escuela.* - They learn Spanish at school.

Beber jugo de limón cada mañana – Drink lemon juice every morning.

Yo *bebo jugo de limón cada mañana.* - I drink lemon juice every morning.

Tú *bebes jugo de limón cada mañana.* - You drink lemon juice every morning.

Usted / **Él** / Ella *bcbe jugo de limón cada mañana.* - He drinks lemon juice every morning.

Nosotros *bebemos jugo de limón cada mañana.* - We drink lemon juice every morning.

Ustedes / **Ellos** (as) *beben jugo de limón cada mañana.* - They drink lemon juice every morning.

Do not forget the pattern for asking and answering questions. Let us review it.

Question:

¿Bebes jugo de limón cada mañana? – Do you drink lemon juice every morning?

Answers:

Si, **bebo** *jugo de limón cada mañana.* – Yes, I drink lemon juice every morning.

No, no **bebo** *jugo de limón cada mañana.* – No, I don't drink lemon juice every morning.

Regular verbs from "Er" Group – Verbos regulares del segundo grupo.

I have listed a few regular verbs from the second group "*ER*" for you to conjugate them and use them in sentences (ask and answers, positive and negative)

Comprender *inglés muy bien* – Understand English very well.

Correr *todos los días* – Run every day.

Creer *en Dios* – Believe in God.

Deber *dinero* – Owe money.

Prender *el fuego* – Light the fire.

Romper *los vasos* – Brake the glasses.

Vender *autos* – Sell cars.

Third Group of verbs (Ir). – Verbos del tercer grupo "Ir".

To conjugate a verb in Spanish you just need to drop the ending or infinitive (*Ir*) and add the corresponding conjugation, which is the same as the second group, the only variation is with "***Nosotros – We***" as you can see below:

Vivir – Live

Yo	viv**o**
Tú	viv**es**
Usted	viv**e**
Él	viv**e**

Ella	viv***e***
Nosotros	viv***imos***
Ustedes	viv***en***
Ellos (as)	viv***en***

Remarks:

As you can see, the conjugation is the same as with the second Group, only one single change in all of them.

Yo viv***o*** en Paris – I live in Paris.

Nosotros viv***imos*** en Alemania – We live in Germany.

Regular verbs from the "Ir" Group – Verbos regulares del grupo "Ir".

I have listed a few regular verbs from the third group "*IR*" for you to conjugate them and use them in sentences (ask and answers, positive and negative)

Abrir *la puerta del carro* – Open the car's door

Aplaudir *al final del discurso* – Applaud at the end of the speech.

Decidir *hablar con Pedro sobre el trabajo* – Decide to speak with Pedro about the job.

Discutir *la situación económica del país* – Discuss about financial situation of the country.

Escribir *un e-mail al profesor de español* – Write an email to the Spanish teacher.

Insistir *en hablar con el director* – Insist to speak with the director.

Partir *para Italia el domingo* – Leave to Italy on Sunday.

Recibir *buenas noticias sobre el curso* – Receive

good news about the course.

Subir las escaleras del apartamento – Go up the stairs of the apartment.

	Ar Group	Er Group	Ir Grupo
Yo	O	O	O
Tú	AS	ES	ES
Usted	A	E	E
Él	A	E	E
Ella	A	E	E
Nosotros	AMOS	EMOS	IMOS
Ustedes	AN	EN	EN
Ellos (as)	AN	EN	EN

Irregular verbs from the three groups – **Verbos irregulares de los tres grupos.**

Conducir el vehículo hasta la casa – **Drive the vehicle back home.**

Yo **conduzco** *el vehículo hasta la casa.* - I drive the vehicle back home.

Tú **conduces** *el vehículo hasta la casa.* - You drive the vehicle back home.

Usted / **Él** / Ella **conduce** *el vehículo hasta la casa.* - He drives the vehicle back home.

Nosotros **conducimos** *el vehículo hasta la casa.* - We drive the vehicle back home.

Ustedes / **Ellos** (as) **conducen** *el vehículo hasta la casa.* - They drive the vehicle back home.

Conocer al profesor de inglés muy bien – **Know the English teacher very well.**

Yo **conozco** al profesor de inglés muy bien. - I know the English teacher very well.

Tú **conoces** al profesor de inglés muy bien. - You know the English teacher very well.

Usted / Él / *Ella* **conoce** al profesor de inglés muy bien. - She knows the English teacher very well.

Nosotros **conocemos** al profesor de inglés muy bien. -   - We know the English teacher very well.

Ustedes / Ellos (as) **conocen** al profesor de inglés muy bien. - You know the English teacher very well.

Dar de comer a los niños hambrientos – Give food to the hungry children (feed).

Yo *doy de comer a los niños hambrientos.* - I give food to the hungry children.

Tú *das de comer a los niños hambrientos.* - You give food to the hungry children.

Usted / *Él* / Ella *da de comer a los niños hambrientos.* - He gives food to the hungry children.

Nosotros *damos de comer a los niños hambrientos.* - We give food to the hungry children.

Ustedes / *Ellos* (as)   *dan de comer a los niños hambrientos.* - They give food to the hungry children.

Decir la verdad todo el tiempo – Tell the truth all the time (Say).

Yo **digo** la verdad todo el tiempo. - I tell the truth all the time.

Tú **dices** la verdad todo el tiempo. - You tell the truth all the time.

Usted / Él / *Ella* **dice** la verdad todo el tiempo. - She tells the truth all the time.

Nosotros **decimos** la verdad todo el tiempo. - We tell the truth all the time.

Ustedes / Ellos (as)   **dicen** la verdad todo el tiempo. - They tell the truth all the time.

Dormir como un bebé – Sleep like a baby.
Yo **duermo** *como un bebé.* - I sleep like a baby.
Tú **duermes** *como un bebé.* - You sleep like a baby.
Usted / Él / Ella **duerme** *como un bebé.* - You sleep like a baby.
Nosotros **dormimos** *como un bebé.* - We sleep like a baby.
Ustedes / **Ellos** (as)   **duermen** *como un bebé.* - They sleep like a baby.
Entender bien el idioma español – Understand well the Spanish Language.
Yo **entiendo** *bien el idioma español.* - I understand well Spanish Language.
Tú **entiendes** *bien el idioma español.* - You understand well Spanish Language.
Usted / **Él** / Ella **entiende** *bien el idioma español.* - He understands well Spanish Language.
Nosotros **entendemos** *bien el idioma español.* - We understand well Spanish Language.
Ustedes / Ellos (as)   **entienden** *bien el idioma español.* - They understand well Spanish Language.

Hacer los ejercicios para aprender mejor – Do the exercises to learn better (Make).
Yo **hago** *los ejercicios para aprender mejor.* - I do the exercises to learn better.
Tú **haces** *los ejercicios para aprender mejor.* - You do the exercises to learn better.
Usted / **Él** / Ella **hace** *los ejercicios para aprender*

mejor. - He does the exercises to learn better.

Nosotros **hacemos** los ejercicios para aprender *mejor.* - We do the exercises to learn better.

Ustedes / **Ellos** (as) **hacen** los ejercicios para aprender mejor. - They do the exercises to learn better.

Ir a la iglesia los domingos – Go to church on Sundays.

Yo **voy** a la iglesia los domingos. - I go to church on Sundays.

Tú **vas** a la iglesia los domingos. - You go to church on Sundays.

Usted / Él / **Ella va** a la iglesia los domingos. - She goes to church on Sundays.

Nosotros **vamos** a la iglesia los domingos. - We go to church on Sundays.

Ustedes / **Ellos** (as) **van** a la iglesia los domingos. - They go to church on Sundays.

Pedir permiso antes de hablar – Ask permission before speaking.

Yo **pido** permiso antes de hablar. - I ask permission before speaking.

Tú **pides** permiso antes de hablar. - You ask permission before speaking.

Usted / Él / Ella **pide** permiso antes de hablar. - You ask permission before speaking.

Nosotros **pedimos** permiso antes de hablar. - We ask permission before speaking.

Ustedes / **Ellos** (as) **piden** permiso antes de hablar. - They ask permission before speaking.

73

Poder comprar el libro de inglés – Be able to buy the English book (Can / May).

Yo *puedo* comprar el libro de inglés. - I can buy the English book.

Tú *puedes* comprar el libro de inglés. - You can buy the English book.

Usted / Él / Ella *puede* comprar el libro de inglés. - She can buy the English book.

Nosotros *podemos* comprar el libro de inglés. - We can buy the English book.

Ustedes / Ellos (as) *pueden* comprar el libro de inglés. - They can buy the English book.

Querer aprender bien el español – Want to learn Spanish.

Yo *quiero* aprender bien el español. - I want to learn Spanish well.

Tú *quieres* aprender bien el español. - You want to learn Spanish well.

Usted / *Él* / Ella *quiere* aprender bien el español. - He wants to learn Spanish well.

Nosotros *queremos* aprender bien el español. - We want to learn Spanish well.

Ustedes / *Ellos* (as) *quieren* aprender bien el español. - They want to learn Spanish well.

Saber hablar en público – Know how to speak in public.

Yo *sé* hablar en público. - I know how to speak in public.

Tú *sabes* hablar en público. - You know how to

speak in public.

Usted / Él / **Ella sabe** *hablar bien en público.* - She knows how to speak well in public.

Nosotros **sabemos** *hablar en público.* - We know how to speak in public.

Ustedes / Ellos (as) **saben** *hablar en público.* - They know how to speak in public.

Salir a ver una película – Go out to watch a movie.

Yo **salgo** *a ver una película.* - I go out to watch a movie.

Tú **sales** *a ver una película.* - You go out to watch a movie.

Usted / **Él** / Ella **sale** *a ver una película.* - He goes out to watch a movie.

Nosotros **salimos** *a ver una película.* - We go out to watch a movie.

Ustedes / **Ellos** (as) **salen** *a ver una película.* - They go out to watch a movie.

Seguir estudiando para aprender bien – Continue studying to learn well.

Yo **sigo** *estudiando para aprender bien.* - I continue studying to learn well.

Tú **sigues** *estudiando para aprender bien.* - You continue studying to learn well.

Usted / Él / **Ella sigue** *estudiando para aprender bien.* - She continues studying to learn well.

Nosotros **seguimos** *estudiando para aprender bien.* - We continue studying to learn well.

Ustedes / **Ellos** (as) **siguen** *estudiando para aprender bien.* - They continue studying to learn well.

Sentir la necesidad de hablar – Feel the need to speak.

Yo *siento* la necesidad de hablar. - I feel the need to speak.

Tú *sientes* la necesidad de hablar. - You feel the need to speak.

Usted / *Él* / Ella *siente* la necesidad de hablar. - He feels the need to speak.

Nosotros *sentimos* la necesidad de hablar. - We feel the need to speak.

Ustedes / Ellos (as) *sienten* la necesidad de hablar. - They feel the need to speak.

Tener mucho trabajo – Have much work.

Yo *tengo* mucho trabajo. - I have much work.

Tú *tienes* mucho trabajo. - You have much work.

Usted / Él / *Ella tiene* mucho trabajo. - She has much work.

Nosotros *tenemos* mucho trabajo. - We have much work.

Ustedes / Ellos (as) *tienen* mucho trabajo. - They have much work.

Traer la comida y la bebida – Bring the food and the drink.

Yo *traigo* la comida y la bebida. - I bring the food and the drink.

Tú *traes* la comida y la bebida. - You bring the food and the drink.

Usted / *Él* / Ella *trae* la comida y la bebida. - He brings the food and the drink.

Nosotros *traemos* *la comida y la bebida.* - We bring the food and the drink.

Ustedes / Ellos (as) *traen* *la comida y la bebida.* - You bring the food and the drink.

Venir a estudiar italiano cada día – Come to study Italian each day.

Yo *vengo* *a estudiar italiano cada día.* - I come to study Italian each day.

Tú *vienes* *a estudiar italiano cada día.* - You come to study Italian each day.

Usted / Él / Ella *viene* *a estudiar italiano cada día.* - She comes to study Italian each day.

Nosotros *venimos* *a estudiar italiano cada día.* - We come to study Italian each day.

Ustedes / Ellos (as) *vienen* *a estudiar italiano cada día.* - They come to study Italian each day.

Ver una película con sus amigos – Watch a movie with one's friends (See).

Yo *veo* *una película con mis amigos.* - I watch a movie with my friends.

Tú *ves* *una película con tus amigos.* - You watch a movie with your friends.

Usted / *Él* / Ella *ve* *una película con sus amigos.* - He watches a movie with his friends.

Nosotros *vemos* *una película con nuestros amigos.* - We watch a movie with our friends.

Ustedes / Ellos (*as*) *ven* *una película con sus amigas.* - They watch a movie with their friends.

You might not have realized it, but you have a very huge knowledge of Spanish so far.

Did you know that you could start speaking Spanish with what you know so far? Why don't you try it?

Mind Game – Juego mental.

Let us play a little mind game to show you how much you already know, but you are not aware of it or you are not using your full capacity on the language. I have placed the answers at the end of the book. Please do not cheat.

How would you say?

I want to know you better.

_____

I don't want to eat today, but I want to drink juice.

_____

Can you bring rice and meat?

_____

Can you give me water?

_____

I cannot give you water, but I can give you beer.

_____

I want to sleep like a baby tomorrow.

_____

She wants to go to the movie, but he doesn't have money.

_____

They want to write an email, but they don't have a computer._____

_____

We want to study Spanish, but we don't have a teacher.

_____

I don't understand Spanish very well. Can you speak in English?_____

_____

A little bit more – Un poco más

Números ordinales - Ordinal numbers

1º - primero – First   2º -   segundo – Second

3º - tercero – Third   4º - cuarto - Fourth
5º - quinto – Fifth   6º - sexto - Sixth
7º - séptimo – Seventh   8º - octavo
9º - noveno   10º - décimo
11º - decimoprimero / undécimo
12º - decimosegundo / duodécimo
13º - decimotercero   14º - decimocuarto
15º - decimoquinto   16º - decimosexto
17º - decimoséptimo   18º - decimoctavo
19º - decimonoveno   20º - vigésimo
21º - vigésimo primero   22º - vigésimo segundo
23º - vigésimo tercero   30º - trigésimo
40º - cuadragésimo   50º - quincuagésimo
60º - sexagésimo   70º - septuagésimo
80º - octogésimo   90º - nonagésimo
100º - centésimo   101º - centésimo primero
200º - ducentésimo   300º - tricentésimo
400° - cuadringentésimo   500°- quingentésimo
600°- sexcentésimo   700°- septingentésimo
800°- octingentésimo   900º - noningentésimo
1000º - milésimo   1000000º - millonésimo

You just need to learn up to 20, since we don't use them very much. However, I have listed all ordinal numbers for your reference.

Enfermedades y síntomas - Diseases and Symptoms

Alergia – Allergy   Alucinar – To hallucinate

Bronquitis – Bronchitis   Cirugía – Surgery

Cirujano – Surgeon   Clínica – Clinic

Congestión – Congestion   Corte – Cut

Dentista – Dentist   Diabetes – Diabetes

Diarrea – Diarrhea   Dolor – Ache, pain

Dolor de estómago – Stomach ache

Dolor de cabeza – Headache   Dolor de oídos – Earache

Enfermedades – Illnesses   Enfermero (a) – Nurse

Fiebre – Fever   Gastroenteritis – Gastroenteritis

Ginecología – Gynecology

Ginecólogo – Gynecologist

Gripe – Flu   Hematología – Hematology

Hemorragia nasal – Nosebleed

Hepatitis – Hepatitis   Herida – Injury

Hospital – Hospital   Infección – Infection

Insomnio – Insomnia   Irritación – Irritation

Maternidad – Maternity hospital

Migraña – Migraine   Náusea – Nausea

Neurólogo – Neurologist

Oculista (oftalmólogo) – Ophthalmologist

Oncología – Oncology   Oncólogo – Oncologist

Otitis – Ear infection   Pediatra – Pediatrician

Pediatría – Pediatrics   Psicólogo – Psychologist

Psiquiatra – Psychiatrist   Psiquiatría – Psychiatry

Resfriado (catarro) – A cold   Reumatismo – Rheumatism

Sala de espera – Waiting room   Síntomas - Symptoms

Temblor – Shivering   Tos – Cough

Vómito – Vomiting

Me duele aquí. – I have a pain here

Me duele el estómago. – I have a stomachache.

Me duele la cabeza. – I have a headache.

Me duelen las muelas. – I have a toothache.

Me encuentro mal. – I feel bad.

Me mareo. – I feel dizzy.

Tengo fiebre. – I have a temperature.

Exercises - Ejercicios

1   Answer the following questions:

¿Dónde vas a comer hoy?

_____

¿Cuándo vas a vender tu carro?

_____

¿Con quién vas a ir a la iglesia el domingo?

_____

¿Vas a venir a casa después del trabajo?

_____

2   Use the correct conjugation of "comer" in the following sentences:

Yo _____ hamburguesas.

Ustedes _____ perros calientes.

Pedro and Pablo _____ manzanas.

3   Use the correct conjugation of "correr" in the following sentences:

Tú _____ todas las mañanas.

Ella _____ con su perro.

Tiffany y yo _____ todas las tardes.

4   Use the correct conjugation of "dormir" in the following sentences:

Ellos _____ con su mama.

Nosotros _____ solos.

Marcos _____ bien.

5   Write down a three line paragraph starting with:

Todos los fines de semana yo_____-

_____

_____

_____

6   Write down a three line paragraph starting

with:

De lunes a Viernes nosotros_____

_____

_____

Reading Comprehension:

¿Cuándo se irá Andrea a Italia? – When is Andrea leaving to Italy?

¿Quién está a dieta? – Who's on a diet?

¿A dónde salió Andrea con el chico de la Iglesia? – Where did Andrea go with the church boy?

Knowledge Base
Republic of Colombia - República de Colombia
Motto: Libertad y Orden - Freedom and Order.
Capital and largest city - Bogotá
Official languages - Spanish
Recognized regional languages - *68 ethnic*

languages and dialects. English also official in the archipelago of San Andrés, Providencia and Santa Catalina.

Demonym - Colombian

Government - Unitary presidential constitutional republic

President - Juan Manuel Santos

Vice President - Germán Vargas Lleras

Population - 48,786,100

Currency - Peso (COP)

Calling code - +57

Bible Verse - Versículo Bíblico

Porque con el corazón se cree para justicia, pero con la boca se confiesa para salvación. **Romanos 10:10.**

Lesson 5 🔒

Mis Compañeros de Clase – My classmates

Mi nombre *es* Alejandro, hoy es mi primer día clases. Hoy *es* catorce de julio del 2016, *son* las 5 de la tarde, llego al salón de clase y me junto con mis compañeros y con el profesor. Su nombre *es* Adam, me han dicho que él *es* muy buen profesor. Se presenta, nos asigna un número a cada uno y nos dice: Cuando llame tu número deberás decir: ¿quién eres?, ¿de dónde *eres*?, ¿qué idioma hablas?, ¿cómo te sientes? Y además algo sobre ti o sobre alguien más de la clase.

1) Yo *soy* Alejandro, *soy* de Colombia, hablo español, *soy* honesto y *estoy* bien.

2) Yo *soy* André, *soy* de Alemania, hablo alemán, *soy* educado y parece que Tiffani y Yeiris *están* enojadas.

3) Yo *soy* Yeiris, *soy* de Noruega y hablo noruego, *soy* inteligente y me parece que el profesor de inglés *está* triste.

4) Yo *soy* Michelle, *soy* de Francia, hablo francés, *soy* profesional y *estoy* enfermo.

5) Yo, *soy* Yeral, soy dominicano, hablo español. Yo *soy* sincero y además *soy* el Pastor de la Iglesia.

6) Yo *soy* Donato, *soy* de Italia y hablo italiano. (Señalando a Niko) Ella *es* mi novia, *es* una mujer muy linda.

7) Yo *soy* Niko, *soy* de China y hablo chino. Donato y yo tenemos un restaurante. El restaurante chino *está* en la calle principal. Si van a visitarnos nosotros *estamos* en la cocina.

8) Yo soy Sonya *soy* de Rusia, hablo ruso, (señalando a Nicolás) Él *es* mi padre, él *es* muy divertido.

9) Yo *soy* Nicolás, *soy* de Brasil, hablo Portugués, *soy* muy sincero y no *estoy* muy bien hoy.

10) Mi nombre *es* Zuri, *soy* de Turquía, hablo turco, *soy* puntual y *estoy* más o menos.

Al terminar de presentarnos, el profesor nos dice: Gracias a todos, *estoy* encantado de conocerlos, *soy* muy responsable. Les recomiendo estos dos libros, el libro de español *es* mío y pienso que *está* muy bien. Quisiera saber por qué todos los estudiantes *están* callados, ojalá no sea que tienen la fiebre del Zica. No, sólo bromeo, deben estar cansados. Mañana tendrán que estar preparados y venir muy contentos. Ya pueden salir.

Word List – Listado dc palabras

Mis Compañeros de Clase – My class mates.
Salón de clase - Classroom.

Me han dicho – I have been told. (12)
Se presenta – Introduces himself.
Nos asigna un número – He assigns us a number.
Y nos dice – And he tells us.

Deberás decir – You will have to say. (10)
O sobre alguien más - Or about someone else.
Pastor de la Iglesia – Pastor of the church.

Dr. Yeral E. Ogando

Señalando a Niko – Pointing at Niko.

Donato y yo tenemos un restaurante – Donato and I have a restaurant.

Si van a visitarnos - If you go to visit us.

Soy puntual – I am punctual.

Más o menos. – More or less.

Les recomiendo estos dos libros – I recommend these two books.

Es mío - Is mine. (8)

*Fiebre del Zica – Zika fever.

Mañana tendrán – You will have tomorrow.

Ya pueden salir. – You may go (You can go out).

Grammar Explanations – Notas gramaticales

We have seen simple present conjugation for all regular verbs and we have seen some main irregular verbs from all the groups as well. We are now ready to start with the main auxiliary verb in Spanish.

The auxiliary verb "Ser o Estar – To be". – El verbo auxiliar "Ser o Estar – To be".

Ser – Be

Yo	soy
Tú	eres
Usted	es
Él	es
Ella	es
Nosotros	somos
Ustedes	son
Ellos (as)	son

Remarks:

There are two verbs with two different uses in Spanish for the verb "To be" as you can see. Make sure you learn how to use them very well, because your success will depend on it.

Whenever you are referring to Origin and Nationality:

Yo soy dominicano y hablo español – I am dominican and I speak Spanish.

Tú eres americano y hablas inglés – You are American and you speak English.

Whenever you are referring to Personality, Physical Attributes, Profession, and Possession.

Él es muy divertido – He is very fun.

Ella es una mujer muy linda – She is a very beautiful woman.

Él es un muy buen profesor – He is a very good teacher.

El libro de español es mío – The Spanish book is mine.

Whenever you are referring to Date and Time.

Son las 5 de la tarde – It is five in the afternoon.

Hoy es catorce de julio del 2016 – Today is July 14th, 2016.

Whenever you are referring to Relationships.

Ella es mi novia – She is my girlfriend.

Él es mi padre - He is my father.

Do not forget the Ask and Answer form.

¿De dónde eres? – Where are you from?

Soy de República Dominicana – I am from Dominican Republic.

*¿Quién **es** usted?* – Who are you?
*Yo **soy** el pastor de la iglesia.* – I am the pastor of the church.

*¿Quién **eres**?* – Who are you?
*Yo **soy** Pedro, ¿y tú?* – I am Pedro, and you?
*Yo **soy** Carmen, encantado de conocerte.* – I am Carmen, nice to meet you.

*¿**Es** ella Dominicana?* – Is she Dominican?
*Si, ella **es** dominicana, pero habla inglés.* – Yes, she is Dominican, but she speaks English.
*No, ella no **es** dominicana, pero habla español.* – No, she is not Dominican, but she speaks Spanish.

List of verbal phrases with "Ser" Lista de frases verbales con "Ser".

Use this list of phrases with *Ser* to practice and master its use.

Ser sincero – Be sincere.
Ser honesto – Be honest.
Ser inteligente – Be intelligent.
Ser profesional – Be professional.
Ser educado – Be educated (polite).
Ser peligroso – Be dangerous.
Ser puntual – Be punctual (on time).
Ser responsable – Be responsible.

The verb "Estar – To be". – El verbo "Estar – To be".

Yo	estoy
Tú	estás
Usted	está
Él	está
Ella	está

Nosotros	estamos
Ustedes	están
Ellos (as)	están

Remarks:
Notice the accent in the second, third person singular and third person plural. It is very important to place the accent always.
Whenever you are referring to Location.
El restaurante chino está en la calle principal – The Chinese restaurant is on the main Street.
Nosotros estamos en la cocina – We are at the kitchen.
Whenever you are referring to Mood and Physical Condition.
El profesor de inglés está triste – The English teacher is sad.
Tiffany y Yeiris están enojadas – Tiffany and Yeiris are angry.
Ustedes están enfermos con la fiebre Zica – You are sick with Zika's fever.
Whenever you are referring to Result of an Action.
Los estudiantes están callados – The students are quiet.
Los profesores están de pie – The teachers are standing.
Please make sure you master these rules before going any further. It might sound very easy to know them. Putting into practice will give you best results.
Always remember the Ask and Answer form.
¿Cómo estás el día de hoy? – How are you today?
Yo estoy muy bien, ¿y usted señor, cómo está

usted? – I am very well, and you Sir, how are you?

No estoy muy bien hoy, pero gracias por preguntar. – I don't feel very well today, but thanks for asking.

¿Cómo estás? – How are you?

Estoy más o menos, ¿y tú? – I am more or less, and you?

Bueno, yo estoy muy bien, gracias. – Well, I am very well, thanks.

List of verbal phrases with "Estar" – List de frases verbales con "Estar".

Use this list of phrases with Estar to practice and master its use.

Estar cansado – Be tired.

Estar contento – Be happy.

Estar triste – Be sad.

Estar enfermo – Be sick.

Estar preparado – Be ready.

Estar perdido – Be lost.

Estar cerrado – Be closed.

Estar abierto – Be opened

Estar limpio – Be cleaned

Estar sucio – Be dirty.

Estar preocupado – Be worried

A Little bit more – Un poco más

Países -	Countries
Alemania	Germany
Armenia	Armenia

Teach Yourself Spanish Level One

Bélgica	Belgium
Bosnia	Bosnia
Brasil	Brazil
Bulgaria	Bulgaria
Cambodia	Cambodia
Canadá	Canada
Colombia	Colombia
Corea del Norte	North Korea
Corea del Sur	South Korea
Croacia	Croatia
China	China
Chipre	Cyprus
Dinamarca	Denmark
Egipto	Egypt
Escocia	Scotland
España	Spain
Estados Unidos	United States
Filipinas	Philippines
Finlandia	Finland
Francia	France
Grecia	Greece
Hungría	Hungary
Inglaterra	England
Irlanda	Ireland
Italia	Italy
Japón	Japan
Malasia	Malaysia
Marruecos	Morocco
Noruega	Norway
Nueva Zelanda	New Zealand
Países Bajos	Netherlands
Polonia	Poland

Portugal	Portugal
Reino Unido	United Kingdom
República Checa	Czech Republic
República Dominicana	Dominican Republic
Rumanía	Romania
Rusia	Russia
Sudáfrica	South Africa
Suecia	Sweden
Suiza	Switzerland
Tailandia	Thailand
Taiwán	Taiwan
Turquía	Turkey
Ucrania	Ukraine
Nacionalidades -	**Nationalities**
Alemán	German
Árabe	Arabian
Bosnio	Bosnian
Búlgaro	Bulgarian
Croata	Croatian
Checo	Czech
Chino	Chinese
Danés	Danish
Escocés	Scottish
Eslovaco	Slovakian
Español	Spanish
Finés	Finnish
Francés	French
Griego	Greek
Hebreo	Hebrew
Holandés	Dutch
Húngaro	Hungarian

Teach Yourself Spanish Level One

Inglés	English
Irlandés	Irish
Italiano	Italian
Japonés	Japanese
Noruego	Norwegian
Polaco	Polish
Portugués	Portuguese
Rumano	Romanian
Ruso	Russian
Serbio	Serbian
Sueco	Swedish
Turco	Turkish
Ucraniano	Ukrainian

Remarks:
Almost 99% of the time, the name of the Language is the same as the nationality, of course in the masculine form.

¿De dónde eres? - Where are you from?

*Soy de **Alemania.*** – I am from Germany.

*Soy **alemán** y hablo **alemán.*** – I am German and I speak German.

¿De dónde eres? – Where are you from?

*Soy **alemana** y hablo **alemán.*** – I am from Germany (female speaking) and I speak German.

Exercises - Ejercicios
Answer the following questions:
1- ¿Cómo estás hoy?

_____

2- ¿De dónde eres?

_____

3- ¿Cuál es la nacionalidad de tu madre?

_____

4- ¿Qué idioma habla tu padre?

_____

5- Complete a three-line paragraph using the verb to be in its form "ser", starting with:

Yo soy Marcos, _____

_____

_____

5- Complete a three-line paragraph using the verb to be in its form "estar", starting with:

Ella está feliz, _____

_____

_____

7- Fill in the following chart:

Country	Language	Nationality
Argentina:	----------------------------	----------------------------

Brasil: -------------------------------- --------------------------------

Francés: -------------------------------- --------------------------------

Italia: -------------------------------- --------------------------------

Japonés: -------------------------------- --------------------------------

Turco: ------------------------------ ----------------------------

Reading Comprehension

1- ¿Qué día es hoy? – What day is today?

2- ¿Cómo están Tiffany y Yeiris? – How are Tiffany and Yeiris?

3- ¿Qué tienen Niko y Donato? – What do Zaco and Donato have?

4- ¿Cómo es Nicolás? – How is Nicolás?

Knowledge Base

Republic of Ecuador - República del Ecuador

Motto: Dios, patria y libertad - God, homeland and freedom.

Capital - Quito

Largest city - Guayaquil

Official languages - Spanish

Recognized regional languages - Kichwa (Quichua), Shuar and others "are in official use for indigenous peoples.

Demonym - Ecuadorian

Government - Unitary presidential constitutional

republic
President - Rafael Correa
Vice President - Jorge Glas
Population - 2015 estimate - 16,144,000
Currency - United States dollar (USD)
Calling code - +593
Sucre until 2000, replaced by the US$ and Ecuadorian centavo coins.
Bible Verse - Versículo Bíblico
Por cuanto todos pecaron, y están destituidos de la gloria de Dios. **Romanos 3:23**

Lesson 6
Cita a Ciegas – Blind date

Hoy tengo una cita a ciegas. Él *se* llama Mario es amigo de mi hermano, nunca lo he visto. Espero que sea lindo, inteligente, simpático y lo más importante de todo: que tenga un gran corazón.

Me preparo desde temprano porque saldremos a almorzar, *me* lavo la cara, *me* baño y *me* lavo la cabeza, quiero oler muy bien. Deseo impresionarle así que voy a ponerme mis mejores ropas ya que para una cita no basta con *ponerse* ropa limpia y voy a *combinarme* con los zapatos rojos que compré la semana pasada. *Me* pongo una falda negra con cremallera, una blusa de seda blanca, medias panti negras, una chaqueta de cuero gris y un hermoso sombrero de algodón con hilos plateados. *Me* peino bien el cabello, *me* maquillo, *me* veo al espejo y creo que estoy muy linda y elegante.

Decido irme caminando, cuando *me* pregunta, ¿*adónde* vamos esta noche? Le digo que *me* gustaría que comamos juntos. Me pregunta entonces, ¿*adónde* podemos ir a cenar? Le hablo del restaurante italiano que queda a tres cuadras de mi casa y acordamos reunirnos allí. *Me* aburro de caminar sola pero estoy alegre porque pronto podré *divertirme* con alguien, espero que Mario sea maravilloso.

Llego al restaurante y estoy perdida *hay* muchos chicos allí. Él *me* dijo qué iba a *ponerse,* así que trato de conseguirlo. Él *se* pone pantalones marrones, camisa manga larga azul y una bufanda blanca y un abrigo con bolsillos de color café. Lo consigo junto a una mesa, no *hay* sillas en la mesa, ¿*por qué* no *hay* sillas en la mesa?, para *asegurarme* le pregunto si él es Mario y *me* responde, sí yo soy el amigo de Héctor.

Él *me* recibe con un beso en la mejilla *me* reconoció por el sombrero que uso. *Me* dice que nos traerán las sillas, cuando llegan con ellas *nos* sentamos. Estoy nerviosa pero emocionada es un chico muy guapo. *Me* pregunta, ¿*cómo* estás hoy? Y le digo que contenta de estar aquí. *Me* pregunta ¿*cuál* es tu nombre? Le digo que Luisana y entonces *me* pregunta *por qué me* llaman Ana si mi nombre es Luisana, le digo que es porque les parece que Luisana es largo. Él *me* dice que Luisana es un hermoso nombre.

Nos traen dos cocteles, uno verde y otro amarillo, son cortesía de la casa, es un caballero y *me* pregunta, ¿quieres tomar?, ¿*cuál* quieres para ti? Le digo que quiero el de color amarillo y *me* lo entrega de inmediato, brindamos. Se acercan a la mesa dos lindas chicas y *nos* saludan, cuando *se* van, le pregunto quiénes son ellas y me dice, ellas son mis hermanas. Después *me* pregunta, ¿*qué* te gusta comer? Y le digo que *me* gusta comer arroz, carne y ensalada, luego *me* pregunta, ¿*qué* quieres tomar? Y le respondo que quiero tomar un jugo de naranja. Él llama al mesero y le pide lo mismo para ambos, dos platos de arroz, carne y ensalada y dos jugos de naranja. *Me* pregunta, ¿*cuánta* azúcar quieres en tu jugo? Y le digo que quiero dos cucharadas, se las pone. Se me queda mirando y me pregunta, ¿*de dónde* eres? Me quedo pensando un rato antes de contestarle que soy de Grecia. Me mira y me dice: excúseme, señorita, ¿*cuándo* piensa usted hablar conmigo? Le contesto, pienso hablar contigo en unos minutos, estoy seca de tantas preguntas que te he contestado.

Le digo, ¿*por qué* preguntas tanto? Y me dice, porque quiero aprender más de ti, ¿*por qué* estás enojada? Y pienso que me ha conquistado con su caballerosidad y dulzura y le digo, no estoy enojada, disfruto de estar aquí contigo. Él sonríe y me pregunta, ¿*qué* piensas hacer hoy? Le digo que hoy pasaré por la Iglesia, se ofrece a *llevarme* en su auto, *se* baja conmigo, asistimos al servicio y luego me deja en casa. ¡Creo que estoy enamorada!

Word List – Listado de palabras

Cita a Ciegas – Blind date.

Nunca lo he visto – I have never seen him. (12)

Espero que sea lindo – I hope he'd be cute. (19)

Y lo más importante de todo – And the most important thing of all.

Que tenga un gran corazón – That he has a good heart.

Almorzar – Have lunch.

Deseo impresionarle – I wish to impress him.

Mis mejores ropas - My best clothes.

No basta – It is not enough.

Voy a combinarme – I will combine (match the clothes).

Compré la semana pasada – I bought last week.

Cremallera – Zipper.

Una blusa de seda blanca – A White silk blouse.

Me veo al espejo - I see myself at the mirror.

Decido irme caminando – I decide to go walking.

Tres cuadras de mi casa – Three blocks away from home.

Divertirme con alguien – Have fun with someone.

Estoy perdida – I am lost.

Qué iba a ponerse así – That it was going to be like that.

Lo consigo junto a una mesa – I found him by the table.

Un beso en la mejilla - A Kiss on the cheek.

Me reconoció – He recognized me.

Un chico muy guapo – A very handsome boy.

Les parece - They think

Es largo – Is long.

Nos traen dos cocteles – They bring us two cocktails.

Son cortesía de la casa – They are on the house.

Él llama al mesero – He calls the waiter.

Se me queda mirando – He stares at me.

Estoy seca – I am dried (tired).

Que te he contestado. – That I have answered.

Aprender más de ti – To learn more of you.

Me ha conquistado – He has conquered me (He has won me).

Su caballerosidad y dulzura – His gentlemanliness and sweetness.

Pasaré por la Iglesia – I will stop by the church (I will go to the church).

¡Creo que estoy enamorada! – I think I am in love.

Grammar Explanations – Notas gramaticales

Let us learn how to use Questions words in Spanish, thus increasing our learning skills and ready to speak Spanish at any time.

Spanish question words. – Palabras de preguntas en español.

¿Cuándo? - When.

*Excúseme, señorita, ¿**cuándo** piensa usted hablar conmigo?* – Excuse me, Miss, when do you think to speak with me?

Pienso hablar contigo en unos minutos – I think to speak with you in a few minutes.

*¿**Cuándo** termina la primera lección del libro?* – When do you finish the first lesson of the book?

Termino la primera lección en 5 minutos – I finish the first lesson in 5 minutes.

¿Adónde? – Where to.

*¿**Adónde** vamos esta noche?* – Where do we go to tonight?

Vamos al cine – We go to the movies.

*¿**Adónde** podemos ir a cenar?* - Where can we go to have dinner?

Podemos ir a cenar al restaurante de la esquina – We can go to the restaurant around the corner.

¿De dónde? – From where.
¿De dónde eres tú? – Where are you from?
Soy de Grecia – I am from Greece.
¿De dónde es usted? – Where are you from?
Soy de Francia – I am from France.

¿Cuántos / Cuántas? – How many (much).
¿Cuántos libros tienes? – How many books do you have?
Tengo dos libros – I have two books.
¿Cuánto dinero necesito? – How much money do you have?
Necesitas 500 Pesos – You need 500 Pesos.
¿Cuántas sillas tenemos? – How many chairs do we have?
Tenemos quince sillas – We have 15 chairs.
¿Cuánta azúcar quieres? – How much sugar do you want?
Quiero dos cucharadas – I want two teaspoon.

¿Qué? - What
¿Qué te gusta comer? – What do you like to eat?
Me gusta comer arroz, carne y ensalada – I like to read rice, meat and salad.
¿Qué quieres tomar? – What do you want to drink?
Quiero tomar un jugo de naranja – I want to drink an orange juice.
¿Qué piensas hacer hoy? – What do you think to do today?
Pienso salir a caminar en el parque – I think to go out and walk in the park.

¿Por qué? Why

¿Por qué preguntas tanto? – Why do you ask so much?

Porque quiero aprender más – Because I want to learn more.

¿Por qué no quieres comer conmigo? – Why you don't want to eat with me?

Porque aún estoy enojado contigo – Because I am still angry with you.

¿Por qué estas enojada? – Why are you angry?

Porque tú no quieres comer conmigo – Because you don't want to eat with me.

¿Cómo? - How.

¿Cómo estás hoy? – How are you today?

Estoy muy bien, gracias – I am very well, thank you.

¿Cómo haces la tarea? – How do you do the homework?

Comienzo por la primera página y la leo bien – I start on the first page and I read it well.

¿Cómo te llamas? – What is your name or how are you called?

Me llamo Luis – My name is Luis or I am called Luis.

¿Cómo te llaman? – What is your name or how are you called?

Me llaman Rey – My name is Rey or I am called Rey.

¿Cuál? – Which.

¿Cuál quieres para ti? – Which one do you want for

you?

Quiero la de color azul – I want the one in blue color.

*¿**Cuáles** zapatos son tuyos?* – Which shoes are yours?

Los zapatos de color rojo son míos – The red color shoes are mine.

*¿**Cuál** es tu nombre?* – What's your name?
Mi nombre es Antonio. – My name is Antonio.

¿Quién? – Who.
*¿**Quién** eres tú?* – Who are you?
Yo soy el amigo de Héctor – I am Hector's Friend.
*¿**Quiénes** son ellas?* – Who are they?
Ellas son mis hermanas – They are my sisters.
*¿**Quién** es él?* – Who is he?
Él es mi mejor amigo – He is my best Friend.

Remarks:
All of the question words take an accent when using them in the interrogative form. You will learn in other lessons that you can use the very same words in non-interrogative form, but without accent.

As you can see, "*Cuánto*" has a singular and plural form for both masculine and feminine.

When using money in a general term it will always be in singular "*Cuánto*", *but when referring to the currency itself, then it is plural "¿**Cuántos** dólares tienes? – How many dollars do you have?.*

When using ¿**Por qué?** In question form See that it is separated into two words and with accent, but if you have noticed when answering it is just one word and without accent "*Porque - Because*".

As you can see when using **¿Cuál - ¿Cuáles?** – **Which.** It has a plural form, but it is the same for masculine and feminine, it does not change. Same rule applies to **¿Quién- Quiénes?** – **Who.**

The verb "To have – Haber (Hay)" – El verbo "To have – Haber (Hay)"

The word "*Hay*" in Spanish represent "**There is and There are**" at the same time in the present tense. It is the only conjugation for the verb "*Haber*". It express the existence of something. *We will see "Haber" as an auxiliary verb in coming units.*

Hay una silla en la sala – There is a chair on the table.

Hay tres libros en la mesa – There are three books on the table.

No *hay* sillas en la mesa – There are no chairs on the table or There isn't any chairs on the table.

¿Por qué no *hay* sillas en la mesa? – Why are there no chairs on the table?

Porque no *hay* sillas en la casa – Because there are no chairs in the house.

As you have learned "*Hay*" works for everything, singular, plural and even for questions.

Reflexive Pronouns - Pronombres Reflexivos.

The reflexive pronouns represent the English "*self*" attached to the personal pronoun "*Myself*". In Spanish is quite different as you can see below:

Personal Pronoun	Reflexive Pronoun
Yo	me

Tú	te
Usted / Él / Ella	se
Nosotros	nos
Ustedes / Ellos (as)	se

Remarks:

Yo me lavo la cabeza – I wash my head (meaning, I wash my head myself).

Tú te lavas la cara – You wash your face.

Usted se baña todos los días – You bathe yourself every day (You take a bath every day).

Él se cambia de ropa para ir a trabajar – He changes clothes to go to work.

Ella se viste de negro para el funeral – She dresses in black for the funeral.

Nosotros nos lavamos bien – We wash ourselves well.

Ustedes se bañan cada noche – You bathe yourself every night (You take a bath every night).

Ellos se bañan mucho – They bathe themselves a lot.

Ellas se bañan mucho – They bathe themselves a lot.

Whenever you see or use the reflexive pronouns, they immediately become the verb into a reflexive verb. Reflexive verbs indicate that the subject of the sentence has performed an action on itself.

As you can see, you always use the personal pronouns when using the reflexive form to identify whom you are referring.

However, with "*Me, Te and Nos*" you can use them

alone.

Me lavo la cabeza (Yo me lavo la cabeza) – I wash my head.

Te lavas la cabeza (Tú te lavas la cabeza) – You wash your head.

Nos lavamos la cabeza (Nosotros nos lavamos la cabeza) - We wash our head.

Reflexive verbs and their conjugations – Verbos reflexivos y sus conjugaciones.

Aburrirse de caminar solo - **Get bored of walking alone.**

Yo me aburro de caminar solo. - I get bored of walking alone.

Tú te aburres de caminar solo. - You get bored of walking alone.

Usted / Él / Ella se aburre de caminar sola. - She gets bored of walking alone.

Nosotros nos aburrimos de caminar solos. - We get bored of walking alone.

Ustedes / Ellos (as) se aburren de caminar solos. - They get bored of walking alone.

Acordarse de la profesora de primaria - **Remember the primary school teacher.**

Yo me acuerdo de la profesora de primaria. – I remember the primary school teacher.

Tú te acuerdas de la profesora de primaria. – You remember the primary school teacher.

Usted / Él / Ella se acuerda de la profesora de primaria. – She remembers the primary school teacher.

Nosotros nos acordamos de la profesora de

primaria. – We remember the primary school teacher.

Ustedes / Ellos (as) **se** *acuerdan de la profesora de primaria.* – They remember the primary school teacher.

Remarks:

Remember that everything must agree with gender and number in Spanish. Make sure to check when you are referring to "**Ella**" and when referring to plural.

Recordarse also means to remember.

Reflexive verbs list – Lista de verbos reflexivos

Here you have a small list of reflexive verbs for you to work with them and learn them better.

Acostarse temprano - Go to bed early.

Afeitarse dos veces por semana - Shave twice per week.

Alegrarse del éxito de alguien - Be glad about the success of someone.

Bañarse bien antes de dormir – Bathe well before sleeping.

Casarse en una iglesia – Get married in a church.

Cepillarse los dientes después de cada comida – Brush one's teeth after every meal.

Convertirse en profesional – Become professional.

Desayunarse cada mañana con frutas - Eat breakfast every morning with fruits.

Despedirse de los compañeros - Say good-bye to one's classmates.

Despertarse cada mañana a las 5 - Wake up every morning at 5 am.

Desvestirse *lentamente* - Get undressed slowly.

Distraerse *mirando la televisión* – Distract oneself watching TV.

Divertirse con alguien - Enjoy oneself with someone.

Dormirse *bien cansado* - Go to sleep very tired.

Ducharse *después de la caminata* – Shower after the walk.

Enfermarse *de repente* - Become ill suddenly.

Enojarse *con alguien* - Get mad with someone.

Graduarse *de la universidad* – Graduate from university.

Irse *de vacaciones* – Leave on vacations.

Lavarse *las manos* – Wash one's hands.

Levantarse *temprano* – Get up early.

Limpiarse *la cara* – Clean one's face.

Mirarse *fijamente* - Look at oneself closely.

Olvidarse *de los problemas* - Forget about the problems.

Pararse *de la silla* – Stand up from the chair.

Peinarse *bien el cabello* - Comb one's hair well.

Ponerse *la ropa limpia* - Put on clean clothes.

Preocuparse *por los problemas* – Worry about problems.

Quitarse *los zapatos después del trabajo* - Take off the shoes after work.

Secarse *bien con la toalla después de ducharse* - Dry off well with the towel after taking a shower.

Sentarse *en la silla del profesor* - Sit down on the teacher's chair.

Subirse *a la cama rápido* - Get up to the bed quickly.

Vestirse para la fiesta - Get dressed for the party.

Reflexive verbs that change their meaning. – Verbos reflexivos que cambian su significado.

Some verbs when becoming a reflexive verb, they change their meaning completely. See some of them below:

Abrir - Open

Abrirse - Open up (confide in someone)

Acordar – Agree

Acordarse - Remember

Cerrar – Close

Cerrarse - Close oneself off emotionally

Combinar - Combine

Combinarse - Take turns

Dormir - Sleep

Dormirse - Fall asleep

Ir - Go

Irse - Go away

Llevar - Carry

Llevarse - Take away *(To listen to someone).*

Poner - Put

Ponerse - Put on / Wear

Salir – Leave

Salirse - Leave unexpectedly / Leak

A Little bit more – Un poco más

Colores - Colors

Amarillo	Yellow
Anaranjado / Naranja	Orange
Azul	Blue

Blanco	White
Café / Marrón	Brown
Dorado	Gold
Gris	Grey
Morado / violeta	Purple
Negro	Black
Plateado	Silver
Rojo	Red
Rosado	Pink
Verde	Green
Ropas -	**Clothing**
Abrigo	Coat
Algodón	cotton
Bata	Dressing-gown
Bikini	Bikini
Blusa	Blouse
Bolsillo	Pocket
Botas	Boots
Botón	Button
Bufanda	Scarf
Camisa	Shirt
Camiseta	T-shirt
Calzoncillos	Underpants
Chaqueta	Jacket
Corbata	Necktie
Cordones	Laces
Correa - Cinturón	Belt
Cremallera	Zipper, zip
Cuero	Leather
Esmoquin	Tuxedo
Falda	Skirt
Franela	Flannel

Gafas de sol	Sunglasses
Gorra	Cap
Guantes	Gloves
Impermeable	Raincoat
Jeans	Jeans
Manga	Sleeve
Medias – Calcetines	Socks
Mini falda	Mini Skirt
Pantalones	Trousers / Pants
Pantalones cortos	Shorts
Pañuelo	Handkerchief
Pijama	Pajamas
Ropa interior	Underwear
Sandalias	Sandals
Seda	Silk
Sombrero	Hat
Sostén / Brasier	Bra
Sudadera	Sweatshirt
Traje	Suit, dress
Uniforme	Uniform
Vestido	Dress
Zapatillas	Slippers
Zapatos	Shoes

Exercises - Ejercicios

1- Answer the following questions:

¿Qué quieres hacer esta tarde?

_____

¿Adónde le gustaría ir a ella?

_____

¿Dónde están las llaves?

_____

¿Cómo haces tu tarea?

_____

¿Cuándo vas a empezar en el nuevo trabajo?

_____

¿Cuáles son tus libros?

_____

¿Cuánto cuesta ese carro?

_____

¿Por qué estás triste?

_____

2-   Create questions with the following sentences:
Voy a comer ensalada.

_____

Él quiere ir al cine.

_____

Está en la gaveta.

_____

Primero saco los ingredientes, después los mezclo y por último los cocino.

_____

El martes por la noche.

_____

Este es mi carro.

_____

Esta manzana cuesta $2.

_____

Están alegres porque están de cumpleaños.

_____

3- Insert the appropriate reflexive forms:

Él _____ hace muchas preguntas a mí.

Ella _____ compra un regalo a él.

Nosotros _____ comemos todas las fresas.

Ellos _____ toman toda la leche.

Tú _____ pones una chaqueta.

Ustedes _____ lavan las manos antes de comer.

Reading Comprehension

1- ¿Quiénes tienen una cita a ciega? – Who have a

blind date?

2- ¿Cómo se va Luisana hasta el restaurante? – How does Luisana go to the restaurant?

3- ¿Adónde van Luisana y Mario después del restaurante? – Where do Luisana and Mario go after the restaurant?

Knowledge Base
Kingdom of Spain - Reino de España
Motto: Plus Ultra - Further Beyond.
Capital and largest city - Madrid
Official language and national language - Spanish
Recognized regional languages - Aragonese Astur-Leonese Basque Catalan Galician Occitan
Demonym - Spanish Spaniard
Government Unitary parliamentary constitutional monarchy
Monarch - Felipe VI
Prime Minister - Mariano Rajoy
Population 2015 census - 46,423,064
Currency – Euro (€) (EUR)
Calling code ı 34
Bible Verse - Versículo Bíblico
Jesús le dijo: Yo soy el camino, y la verdad, y la vida; nadie viene al Padre, sino por mí. **Juan 14:6**

Lesson 7 🔒

¿Me Opero o no me Opero? - Do I need surgery?

Mi nombre es Emilia, tengo 18 años de edad, estudio diseño de modas y soy modelo. Aunque todos dicen que soy linda, creo que necesito muchos arreglos, así que *estoy decidiendo* si hacerme una cirugía estética. He decidido reunirme con mi amiga Carla a ver qué opina ella.

Me dijo que estará *llegando* a mi casa a las tres de la tarde, sólo faltan diez minutos para que llegue. Me quedo en el salón familiar *pensando* qué voy a decirle, espero que esté de acuerdo conmigo y me ayude a tomar la decisión de operarme.

Está *sonando* el timbre, debe ser ella, voy a abrir y allí está.

Emilia: Hola Carla, gracias por venir.

Carla: Hola amiga, traje algo de comida para que comamos y bebamos juntas mientras estamos *hablando*.

Emilia: Perfecto, ven vamos a sentarnos en la cocina.

Carla: Me interesa escucharte, dime qué es tan urgente, me estoy *muriendo* de miedo, no podía creer que estuvieras pidiéndome ayuda cuando sé que eres tan independiente.

Emilia: Todo bien, sólo quiero tu consejo. Cuéntame quién iba conduciendo tu auto.

Carla: Era Julián, un compañero de clase, el suyo se dañó y me pidió prestado el mío, me duele la cabeza de sólo pensar que me lo vaya a chocar.

Emilia: Estoy segura de que todo irá bien. Bueno voy al punto, sabes que no me gusta mi nariz, tampoco me gusta mi barriga y mucho menos me gusta mi pelo. Con el pelo no he tenido problema pues bastó con pintármelo. Pero lo de la nariz y la barriga es otra cosa.

Carla: Por favor, eres preciosa, Dios te ha bendecido con un rostro hermoso y un cuerpo despampanante, no me digas que te quieres operar.

Emilia: Pues sí.

Carla: Pienso que te estás ***buscando*** problemas, vienes ***pensando*** en tonterías desde que decidiste hacerte modelo.

Emilia: Entiéndeme, todas las otras chicas en la academia de modelaje son perfectas y yo no lo soy.

Carla: Nadie es perfecto Emilia. Sabes que pienso que eres preciosa, tienes un hermoso cabello castaño, unos lindos ojos negros, una nariz diminuta, una boca generosa, unas orejas muy lindas, un cuello largo y delgado, un hermoso busto, una cintura delgada, unas caderas curvilíneas y piernas bien torneadas. Considero que no hay nada que tengas que hacerte para ser más bella de lo que eres.

Emilia: ¿Es realmente eso lo que piensas? ¿No estás mintiéndome?

Carla: Claro que no, me molesta que lo creas y que siquiera pienses en esa cirugía que en el peor de los casos podría hacerte caer en coma, además no cuentas con el dinero para eso. Y en cuanto a la pregunta que me estás haciendo, puedo decirte que tú me conoces y sabes que no miento. Estaba *pensando* que sería mejor que le dediques más tiempo a tus estudios y a tu crecimiento interior para que dejes de preocuparte por cosas que realmente no valen la pena.

Emilia: Amiga tienes razón, me quedo como soy, no voy a operarme, te haré caso y me dedicaré a cosas que realmente son importantes.

Word List – Listado de palabras

¿Me Opero o no me Opero? – Do I get a surgery or not?

Tengo 18 años de edad – I am 18 years old.

Diseño de modas - Fashion design.

Modelo. – Model.

Cirugía estética – Cosmetic Surgery.

Estará llegando – She is arriving.

Tomar la decisión - Make a decision.

De operarme – To have a surgery.

El timbre – The doorbell

Debe ser ella – It must be her.

Traje algo de comida – I brought some food.

Dime qué es tan urgente – Tell me what is the urgency.

Que estuvieras pidiendome - That you would be asking me. (14)

Sólo quiero tu consejo – I just want an advise.

Iba conduciendo - I was driving.

El suyo se dañó - His got broken.

Me pidió prestado – And he borrowed.

De sólo pensar - Of only thinking.

Que me lo vaya a chocar – That he might crash it.

Bueno voy al punto – Well, let's get to the point.

Mi barriga – My belly.

Dios te ha bendecido – God has blessed you.

Un cuerpo despampanante – An stunning body.

Entiéndeme – Understand me.

Una nariz diminuta – A tiny nose.

Una boca generosa – A generous mouth (beautiful mouth).

Un cuello largo y delgado – And long and thin neck.

Un hermoso busto – A nice breast.

Unas caderas curvilíneas – A curved hips.

Piernas bien torneadas – Well shape legs.

Que siquiera pienses – That you even think. (That you even consider).

En el peor de los casos - In the worst of the cases (In the worst scenario).

Además no cuentas con el dinero – Besides, you don't have the money.

Crecimiento interior – Inner growth.

Me dedicaré – I will dedicate myself.

☑ Grammar Explanations – Notas gramaticales

🔒 The Gerund – El Gerundio.

The Gerund or better known in English as "ing" is used to express several continuous actions in Spanish.

To form the gerund or Ing in Spanish, just drop

the infinite of the verbs *"Ar – Er – Ir"* and add the proper ending as expressed below.

For verbs of the first group "Ar", just add "ANDO".

Hablar - Hablando

Lavar - Lavando

For verbs of the second and third group "Er – Ir", just add "IENDO".

Comer – Comiendo

Beber – Bebiendo

There is no change in gender or number with this time, it always remain the same.

In English, you need the verb *"To be"* to use *"Ing"* in Spanish, you need the verb *"Estar".* Please *remember the conjugation of "Estar".*

Yo	estoy	hablando
Tú	estás	hablando
Usted	está	hablando
Él	está	hablando
Ella	está	hablando
Nosotros	estamos	hablando
Ustedes	están	hablando
Ellos (as)	están	hablando

Remarks:

As you can see the gerund does not change, just the combination of *"estar"* makes the changes.

*Yo **estoy hablando** por teléfono* – I am speaking on the phone.

*Tú **estás comiendo** arroz* – You are eating rice.

*Usted **está escribiendo** una carta en inglés – You are writing a letter in English.*

*Él **está bebiendo** jugo de limón* – He is drinking

lemon juice.

Ella está jugando en el jardín – She is playing at the garden.

Nosotros estamos escuchando música – We are listening to music.

Ustedes están escuchando la radio – You are listening to the radio.

Ellos (as) están cocinando arroz con carne – They are cooking rice with meat.

Remember, these actions are actually happening at the very same moment.

Changing verbs in the Gerund – Verbos cambiantes al Gerundio.

Verbs that end in two vowels or whose word stem ends with a vowel *"Er – Ir"* take *"YENDO"* to form the gerund.

Leer un libro – Read a book.

Leyendo un libro – Reading a book.

Estamos leyendo un libro de historia – We are reading a history book.

Creer en Dios – Belive in Cod.

Creyendo en Dios – Believing in God.

Ella está creyendo en Dios por el sermón – She's believing in God because of the sermon.

Oír un sonido – Hear a sound.

Oyendo un sonido – Hearing a sound.

Estoy oyendo un sonido extraño – I am hearing a strange sound.

Caer en coma – Fall in coma.

Cayendo en coma – Falling in coma.

La paciente está cayendo en coma – The patient is

falling into a coma.

Traer la comida – Bring food.

Trayendo la comida – *Bringing food.*

Mi hijo **está trayendo** *la comida, espere un momento* – My son is bringing the food, wait a momento.

Irregular verbs in the Gerund – Verbos irregulares al Gerundio.

There are some irregular verbs in the gerund; they do not follow any pattern, so you have to learn them by heart.

Pedir ayuda – Ask for help

Pidiendo ayuda – Asking for help.

Ustedes **están pidiendo** *ayuda para los niños huérfanos* – You are asking for help for orphan children.

Sentir bendecido – Feel blessed

Sintiendo bendecido – Feeling blessed.

Hoy me **estoy sintiendo** *bendecido* – Today I am feeling blessed.

Decir mentiras – Tell / Say lies

Diciendo mentiras – Telling / Saying lies.

Ella **está diciendo** *muchas mentiras* – She is telling many lies.

Dormir muy bien – Sleep very well

Durmiendo muy bien – Sleeping very well.

Ellas **están durmiendo** *muy bien* – They are sleeping very well.

Morir del miedo – Die of fear

Muriendo del miedo – Dying of fear.

Me **estoy muriendo** *del miedo* – I am dying of fear.

Teach Yourself Spanish Level One

Do not forget the Ask and Answer form.

¿Qué estás haciendo? – What are you doing?

Estoy escribiendo un libro de poesía – I am writing a poetry book.

No estoy haciendo nada – I am doing nothing (I am not doing anything).

¿Estás hablando conmigo? – Are you talking to me?

Sí, estoy hablando contigo. – Yes, I am talking to you.

No, no estoy hablando contigo. – No, I am not talking to you.

¿Por qué estamos hablando del tema? – Why are we speaking about the subject?

Estamos hablando del tema porque tú aún no me entiendes – We are speaking about the subject because you still do not understand me.

The gerund with the verb "Ir" – El gerundio con el verbo "Ir".

Did you know that you could also use the gerund with "*Ir*"?

By doing so, you will sound like a native speaker. Whenever you use it with the gerund it will it often express surprise, confusion, or a little more emotion. You can use it to express actions that are gradually unfolding over time too.

¿Quién va conduciendo el carro? – Who is driving the car?

Mi hija va poco a poco *convirtiéndose* en toda una mujer – My daughter is Little by Little becoming a woman.

The gerund with the verbs "Andar / Venir" – El gerundio con los verbos "Andar / Venir".

You can also use the gerund with "Andar – Venir" giving the idea of a repeated or insistent action.

Haití anda siempre teniendo apagones – Haiti is always having blackouts.

Maritza viene buscando problemas en la mañana – Maritza comes looking for problems in the morning.

The verb "To like – Gustar" – El verbo "Gustar".

The verb "*Gustar – Like*" in Spanish. This verb can be very confusing for English speaker, that's why I am creating this section special for "Gustar – Like".

Check this out. In English you say "*I like to eat*" but in Spanish you cannot say *"Yo gusto comer"*, if you do so, you will sound like a Caveman trying to speak the language. The reason why this verb is conjugated like this is *because instead of directly meaning* like, **it actually means that something is pleasing for you**. See below:

Me gusta – I like

Te gusta – You like

Le gusta – You (polite) / He likes / She likes.

Nos gusta – We like.

Les gusta - You (plural) / They like.

Remarks:

Me gusta *comer helado* – I like to eat ice cream.

Nos gusta *mucho ir al cine* – We like very much to go to the movies.

Te gusta *trabajar en la tienda* – You like to work on the store.

As you can see, *"gusta"* does not change, however there is a plural version when you are speaking about more than one thing.

Me gustan – I like

Te gustan – You like

Le gustan – You (polite) / He likes / She likes.

Nos gustan – We like.

Les gustan - You (plural) / They like.

Me gustan los caballos – I like horses.

Nos gustan las películas de acción – We like action movies.

To give more emphasis and indentify the person who you are referring to, we use a propositional phrase before the *"Me gusta"*

A *mí* me gusta comer – I like to eat.

A *tí* te gusta trabajar – You like to work.

A *usted* le gusta estudiar – You (formal) like to study.

A *él* le gusta cantar – He likes to sing.

A *ella* le gusta bailar - She likes to dance.

A *nosotros* nos gusta orar – We like to pray.

A *ustedes* les gusta predicar   You (plural) like to preach.

A *Ellos (as)* les gusta leer – They like to read.

As you can see, the English translation is the same, however, in Spanish it has more emphasis and you can also know exactly who you are referring to, instead of confusing one person with another.

Do not forget that it is the same with the plural.

A *mí* me *gustan* las películas de acción – I like action movies.

Always remember the Ask and Answer form.

¿Qué te gusta comer? – What do you like to eat?

Me gusta comer arroz con habichuela, pollo frito y ensalada – I like to eat rice and beans, fried chicken and salad.

¿Le gusta a él escuchar música? – Does he like to listen to music?

Si, a él le gusta escuchar música. - Yes, he likes to listen to music.

No, a él no le gusta escuchar música. - No, he doesn't like to listen to music.

¿Te gustan las manzanas? – Do you like apples?

No, no me gustan las manzanas – No, I don't like apples.

Sí, me gustan las manzanas – Yes, I like apples.

¿Le gusta a ella ir de tiendas? – Does she like to go shopping?

Si, a ella le gusta ir de compras – Yes, she likes to go shopping.

No, a ella no le gusta ir de compras – No, she doesn't like to go shopping.

¿Les gustan a ellos las chicas inteligentes? – Do they like smart girls?

Si, a ellos les gustan las chicas inteligentes – Yes, they like smart girls.

No, a ellos no les gustan las chicas inteligentes – No, they don't like smart girls.

Did you notice how easy is to construct the negative form?

You just need to place "No" between the prepositional phrase *"A mí – A tí - A él..."* and the

Indirect Object Pronoun "*Me – te – le...*" or simply before the *"Me – te – le..."*

Other verbs like "Gustar" – Otros verbos como "Gustar".

Some other verbs take the same pattern as "Gustar". I am listing some of them here for your practice and better learning experience.

Doler la cabeza – Pain in the head (Head hurts – Headache).

Me duele la cabeza – I have a headache.

Encantar la música en español – Love (like) Spanish music.

A él le encanta la música en español – He loves Spanish music.

Faltar dinero de la cartera – Miss money from the wallet (purse).

A ella le falta dinero de la cartera – She misses money from the purse.

Interesar los libros bíblicos – Be interested in Bible books.

A ellos les interesan los libros bíblicos – They are interested in Bible books.

Molestar la música alta – Bother loud music.

A ustedes les molesta la música alta – Loud music bothers you.

Quedar tranquilo – Remain quiet / Calm.

Me quedo tranquilo siempre cuando hay problemas – I always remain calm when there are problems.

Quedar bien – Fit (suit) well (when wearing something).

*Ese vestido **te queda** muy bien* – That dress suits you very well.

More irregular verbs – Más verbos irregulares.
Bendecir la comida – Bless the meal.
*Yo **bendigo** la comida.* – I bless the meal.
*Tú **bendices** la comida.* – You bless the meal.
*Usted / Él / **Ella bendice** la comida.* - She blesses the meal.
*Nosotros **bendecimos** la comida.* – We bless the meal.
*Ustedes / **Ellos** (as) **bendicen** la comida.* – They bless the meal.

Contar el dinero – Count the money.
*Yo **cuento** el dinero.* – I count the money.
*Tú **cuentas** el dinero.* – You count the money.
*Usted / **Él** / Ella **cuenta** el dinero.* – He counts the money.
*Nosotros **contamos** el dinero.* – We count the money.
*Ustedes / **Ellos** (as) **cuentan** el dinero.* – They count the money.

Elegir el próximo presidente – Elect (Choose) the next president.
*Yo **elijo** el próximo presidente.* – I elect the next president.
*Tú **eliges** el próximo presidente.* – You elect the next president.
*Usted / Él / **Ella elige** el próximo presidente.* - She elects the next president.
*Nosotros **elegimos** el próximo presidente.* – We elect the next president.

*Ustedes / **Ellos** (as)*   ***eligen***   *el*   *próximo presidente.* – They elect the next president.

Jugar béisbol en el estadio – Play baseball at the stadium.

*Yo **juego** béisbol en el estadio.* – I play Baseball at the stadium.

*Tú **juegas** béisbol en el estadio.* – You play Baseball at the stadium.

*Usted / **Él** / Ella   **juega** béisbol en el estadio.* He plays Baseball at the stadium.

*Nosotros **jugamos** béisbol en el estadio.* – We play Baseball at the stadium.

*Ustedes / **Ellos** (as)*   ***juegan***   *béisbol en el estadio.* – They play Baseball at the stadium.

Mover la cabeza de uno – Move one's head.

*Yo **muevo** mi cabeza.* – I move my head.

*Tú **mueves** tu cabeza.* – You move your head.

*Usted / **Él** / Ella   **mueve** su cabeza.* – He moves his head.

*Nosotros **movemos** nuestras cabezas.* – We move our heads.

*Ustedes / **Ellos** (as)*   ***mueven***   *sus   cabezas.* – They move their heads.

Sonreír aun cuando estás triste – Smile even when you are sad.

*Yo **sonrío** aun cuando estoy triste.* – I smile even when I am sad.

*Tú **sonríes** aun cuando estás triste.* – You smile even when you are sad.

*Usted / Él / **Ella**   **sonríe** aun cuando está triste.* – She smiles even when she is sad.

*Nosotros **sonreímos** aun cuando estamos tristes.* –

We smile even when we are sad.

Ustedes / Ellos (as) **sonríen** *aun cuando están tristes.* – You smile even when you are sad.

A Little bit more – Un poco más

Partes del cuerpo - Body parts

Amígdalas	Tonsils
Arteria	Artery
Boca	Mouth
Brazo	Arm
Cabeza	Head
Cadera	Hip
Cara	Face
Codo	Elbow
Columna vertebral	Spinal cord
Corazón	Heart
Costilla	Rib
Cuello	Neck
Dedo	Finger
Dedo del pie	Toe
Diente	Tooth
Espalda	Back
Estomago	Stomach
Garganta	Throat
Hígado	Liver
Hombro	Shoulder
Hueso	Bone
Intestino	Intestine
Labio	Lip
Lengua	Tongue
Mandíbula	Jaw

Mano	Hand
Muñeca	Wrist
Músculo	Muscle
Nariz	Nose
Nervio	Nerve
Ojo	Eye
Oreja	Ear
Pecho	Chest
Pelo	Hair
Pie	Foot
Piel	Skin
Pierna	Leg
Pulgar	Thumb
Pulmón	Lung
Riñón	Kidney
Rodilla	Knee
Tendón	Tendon
Tobillo	Ankle
Vena	Vein
Vesícula	Bladder

Exercises - Ejercicios

1- Use the se verbs in their gerund form to complete the following text:

Yo estoy__ *ir*__ a la escuela en este momento. Voy a recoger a mi hija, puedo verla, ella está __*jugar*__ con una amiguita con la que está __*estudiar*__ ballet. Ellas están __*hacer*__ castillos de arena. Puedo ver que se están __*ensuciar*__el uniforme, pero no importa porque se están __*divertir*__ muchísimo.

2- Express the activities that each member of your family likes to or does not like to do, using the verb "gustar".

A mí _____ _____ comer _____.

A ellos no _____ _____ comer _____.

A mí mamá _____ _____ beber _____.

A él no _____ _____ tomar _____.

A mis hijos _____ _____ jugar _____.

A nosotros _____ _____ jugar _____.

3- Draw the silhouette of a person and indicate where the following parts are: quijada, costillas, muñecas, rodillas and talones.

Reading comprehension

1- ¿Cómo se llama la amiga de Emilia? – What's the name of Emilia's Friend?

2- ¿Qué quiere hacerse Emilia? – What does Emilia want to do?

3- ¿Qué le aconseja Carla? – What does Carla advise her?

Knowledge Base

Republic of Guatemala - República de Guatemala

Motto: El País de la Eterna Primavera - The Land of the Eternal Spring.

Capital and largest city - Guatemala City

Official language - Spanish

Demonym - Guatemalan

Government - Unitary presidential republic

President - Jimmy Morales

Vice President - Jafeth Cabrera

Population - 2014 estimate - 15,806,675

Currency - Quetzal (GTQ)

Calling code - +502

Bible Verse - Versículo Bíblico

Porque no envió Dios a su Hijo al mundo para condenar al mundo, sino para que el mundo sea salvo por él. **Juan 3:17.**

Lesson 8

Su Cumpleaños – His birthday

Victoria: Dios *mío*, ya son las siete en punto de la mañana. Helena, ¿Se fue Rafael?

Helena: Sí señora, dijo que almorzará *en su* oficina al medio día y regresará temprano en la tarde.

Victoria: Me siento mal, anteayer visité *mi* médico, seguí *su* tratamiento, pero no siento mejoría y yo sin preparar el cumpleaños *de* Rafael.

Helena: ¿Por qué no ordena *su* cena a la agencia de festejos?

Victoria: *tu* idea es magnífica. Ordenaré *nuestra* cena para veinte personas, que incluya aquel plato de mariscos, *su* preferido y *su* torta *de* cumpleaños con *sus* treinta velitas. Rafael tendrá *su* celebración.

Helena: Señora, ¿corto varias de esas flores olorosas que tiene en *su* jardín?

Victoria: Si, gracias por *tu* ayuda, confeccionaré un arreglo para *nuestra* mesa del comedor; pondré en el salón la mesa pequeña de mi hermana Mary para la torta y le pondré aquel mantel que me tejió mamá; *mi* padre que es tan simpático, le recordará a nuestros invitados.

Helena: ¿Y *su* regalo señora?

Victoria: Aquel paquete que traje el otro día, es este bonito libro azul que habla de *nuestra* historia y *nuestros* héroes, este es uno de **sus** temas preferidos.

Helena: ¿Quienes vienen señora?

Victoria: *Nuestros* familiares y aquellos amigos allegados.

Helena: El perro de *su* hermano Juan ha ladrado mucho,

Victoria: veré que pasa. Juan, hermano, *tu* perro les está ladrando a esos tres hombres que están en la esquina, ¿son esos hombres peligrosos?

Juan: No, no lo son. Mira quería preguntarte sí aquella mujer de pelo largo es bruta, se ha caído dos veces.

Victoria: ella es *nuestra* nueva vecina, esa chica es muy inteligente, tal vez un poco torpe en *su* andar, *sus* piernas son dos prótesis, tiene dos hermanas, esas mujeres son atractivas. Qué bueno es tenerte al lado, nos vemos por la noche,

Juan: en el cumpleaños *de* Rafael.

Victoria: Usaré ese pantalón rojo que es *mío* con *mi* blusa *de* seda negra,

Helena: elegante esa combinación.

Rafael: Ya llegué,

Victoria: Feliz cumpleaños *mi* amor, tendrás *tu* torta esta noche.

Pedro: ¿Es esta la casa de la señora Victoria? Vengo de la agencia de festejos.

Helena: Si, esta es.

Pedro: le traigo *su* pedido, incluyendo la torta para su esposo.

Helena: Colocaremos la torta, esta mesa pequeña y las fuentes con la cena en aquella mesa grande de *su* comedor.

Victoria: son las ocho en punto, nuestros invitados están por llegar,

Rafael: viene entrando un señor y dos damas,

Victoria: ese es *mi* profesor de pintura,

Rafael: ¿La señora es *su* mamá?

Victoria: Si, ella es la mamá de *mi* profesor y la chica rubia es *su* hermana. ¡Llegó nuestra familia! Mamá ese vestido es lindo, esa falda que trae Mary es *mía.*

Mary: pero ahora es *nuestra*, la mesa para la torta te quedo bellísima,

Victoria: esa mesa es **tuya.**

Rafael: ¿Faltan invitados tuyos?

Victoria: Si, **tus** compañeros de trabajo que llegan en esa camioneta y en ese lindo carro negro viene *tu* jefe con *su* esposa Martha y *su* bebé.

Rafael: ¿Están todos aquí ya? Son las ocho y diez,

Victoria: si, todos a tiempo.

Marta: La casa de ustedes es linda y grande,

Rafael: gracias.

Martha: ¿Podría acostar a mi bebé que está dormido?

Victoria: Si, la habitación de al lado, tiene *su* cama de dormir para nuestros huéspedes.

Marta: gracias.

Victoria: Pasemos al comedor ahora, ó nuestra cena se enfría.

Rafael: Gracias por esta exquisita cena y su compañía.

Victoria: Acompañemos todos a Rafael a apagar *sus* treinta velitas a las diez en punto, hora de *su* nacimiento.

Todos: Cumpleaños feliz, te deseamos a ti, cumpleaños Rafael, cumpleaños feliz.

Word List – Listado de palabras
Su Cumpleaños – His birthday.

Anteayer visité mi médico – Day before yesterday I visited the doctor.

Seguí su tratamiento – I followed his treatment.

Tu idea es magnífica – Your idea is terrific.

Su preferido – His favorite.

Rafael tendrá su celebración – Rafael will have his celebration.

Flores olorosas - Flowers with scents (Smelly flowers).

Confeccionaré un arreglo – I will prepare a gift (present).

Que me tejió mamá – That Mom wove me.

Nuestros héroes – Our heroes.

De sus temas preferidos – Of his favorites subjects (topics).

Amigos allegados – Close Friends.

Ha ladrado mucho – Has barked a lot.

Veré que pasa – I will see what happen.

Mira quería preguntarte – Look, I'd wanted to ask you. (9)

Se ha caído dos veces – She has fallen twice.

Nueva vecina – New neighbor.

Un poco torpe en su andar – A little clumsy on her walk.

Dos prótesis – Two prosthesis

Ya llegué – I arrived already.

Agencia de festejos – Party agency.

Nuestros invitados están por llegar – Our guests are about to arrive.

Un señor y dos damas – A gentleman and two ladies.

En esa camioneta – In that van.

Si, todos a tiempo – yes, all on time.

La habitación de al lado – Next door room.

Exquisita cena - Exquisit dinner.

Apagar sus treinta velitas – Blow off his 30 candles.

Hora de su nacimiento – The time of his birth.

✒️ Grammar Explanations – Notas gramaticales

🔒 Possessive adjectives – Adjetivos posesivos.

When you want to say whom something belongs. Possessive adjectives do just that by indicating which person possesses or owns it. Possessive adjectives are used to show ownership.

Singular	Plural	
Mi	Mis	My
Tu	Tus	Your
Su	Sus	your (polite), his, her, its
Nuestro (a)	Nuestros (as)	our
Su	Sus	Their

Remarks:

As you can see there is a plural form for each one of them, of course, the plural is for when you are referring to more than one thing. "*Mi* - *Tu* – *Su*" do not have masculine and feminine forms. They stay the same, regardless of the gender of the nouns they modify.

When using them it does not make any distinction if the possessed object is feminine or masculine, they all remain the same with the exception of *"Nuestro".*

Mi carro es negro - My car is black.

Mis carros son negros – My cars are black.

Tu libro es muy bonito – My book is very beautiful.

Tus libros son muy bonitos – Your books are very beautiful.

If you have noticed *"tu"* does not have accent, it only takes the accent when you are referring to the personal pronoun "*You*".

The tricky part is with "Su – Sus" because it can refer to five different pronouns.

Su casa es linda – Your (polite) house is beautiful.

Su casa es linda – His house is beautiful.

Su casa es linda – Her house is beautiful.

Su casa es linda. – Your house is beautiful.

Su casa es linda – Their house is beautiful.

As you can see, the same sentence means five different things in Spanish, it looks confusing, isn't it? Well, it is not, let us now simplify the process.

Because we want to make sure people understand whom we are referring, we are going to substitute the possessive adjective by prepositional phrase "*De* – *Of*" plus the personal pronoun.

Su casa es linda – Your (polite) house is beautiful.

La casa de usted es linda. (Literal. **The house of you is beautiful**).

Su casa es linda – His house is beautiful.

La casa de él es linda.

Su casa es linda – Her house is beautiful.

La casa de ella es linda.

Su casa es linda. – Your house is beautiful.

La casa de ustedes es linda.

Su casa es linda – Their house is beautiful.

La casa de ellos (as) es linda -

The only possessive adjective that has four forms is "Nuestro - Our"

Nuestro vaso es rojo – Our glass is red. (Masculine Singular).

Nuestros vasos son rojos – Our glasses are red. (Masculine Plural).

Nuestra casa es grande – Our house is big. (Feminine Singular).

Nuestras casas son grandes – Our houses are big. (Feminine Plural).

The possessive case "Of / 'S – De" – El caso posesivo "Of / 'S – De".

You have also learnt the Possessive Case "*De - of / 'S*". In English, you can say:

The house of John or John's house. Both sentences mean the same in Spanish, we only use "*De - of*"

La casa de Juan – The house of John or John's house.

El perro de María – The dog of Maria or Maria's

dog.

You just need to place "*De - of*" before the possessor.

Do not forget the Ask and Answer form.

¿Es tu casa linda? – Is your house pretty?

Si, mi casa es linda. – Yes, my house is pretty.

No, mi casa no es linda. – No, my house is not pretty.

¿Es nuestro padre simpático? – **Is our father funny?**

Si, nuestro padre es simpático. – Yes, our father is funny.

No, nuestro padre no es simpático. – No, our father is not funny.

Demonstrative Adjectives – Adjetivos demostrativos.

In Spanish, there are 3 sets of demonstrative adjectives and they demonstrate a quality about the noun they modify. The location in respect to the speaker or the listener is essential when learning "*This – These / That - Those*" Please note that each one has a "*Singular, Plural, Masculine and Feminine*" form.

Masculine Singular	Masculine Plural
Este – This	*Estos* - These

Este carro es lindo - *This* car is beautiful.

Estos carros son lindos - These cars are beautiful.

Este libro es bueno – This book is good.

Estos libros son buenos – These books are good.

Feminine Singular	Feminine Plural
Esta – This	*Estas* - These

Esta casa es hermosa – This house is pretty.

Estas casas son hermosas – These houses are pretty.

Esta mesa es grande – This table is big.

Estas mesas son grandes - These tables are big.

Remember, it is used to point out nouns that are close the speaker as well as the person to whom he or she is speaking and within the reaching distance.

Masculine Singular	Masculine Plural
Ese – That	**Esos** – Those

Ese vestido es lindo – That dress is pretty.

Esos vestidos son lindos – Those dresses are pretty.

Ese señor es feo – That man is ugly.

Esos señores son feos – Those men are ugly.

Feminine Singular	Feminine Plural
Esa – That	**Esas** – Those

Esa mujer es muy atractiva – That woman is very attractive.

Esas mujeres son muy atractivas – Those women are very attractive.

Esa chica es muy inteligente – That girl is very intelligent.

Esas chicas son muy inteligentes – Those girls are very intelligent.

Remember, it is used to point out nouns that are further from the speaker and not easily within reach. The noun may be close to the listener, but not the speaker.

Masculine Singular -	Masculine Plural
Aquel – That over there	**Aquellos** – Those over there.

Aquel libro es azul – That book over there is blue.

Aquellos libros son azules – Those books over there are blue.

Aquel chico está enfermo – That boy over there is sick.

Aquellos chicos están enfermos – Those boys over there are sick.

Feminine Singular - Feminine Plural

Aquella – That over there   **Aquellas** – Those over there.

Aquella mujer está trabajando – That woman over there is working.

Aquellas mujeres están trabajando – Those women over there are working.

Aquella flor es olorosa – That flower over there smells good.

Aquellas flores son olorosas – Those flowers over there small good.

Remember, it is used to point out nouns that are far away from both the speaker and the listener, but within visual distance.

Do not forget the Ask and Answers form.

¿Es este tu libro? – Is this your book?

Si, este es mi libro. – Yes, this is my book.

No, este no es mi libro. – No, this is not my book.

¿Son estos tus libros? – Are these your books?

Si, estos son mis libros. – Yes, these are my books.

No, estos no son mis libros. – No, these are not my books.

¿Es esta la casa de ella? – Is this her house?

Si, esta es la casa de ella. – Yes, this is her house.

No, esta no es la casa de ella. – No, this is not her house.

¿Son estas las flores de ellos? – Are these their flowers?

Si, estas son las flores de ellos. – Yes, these are their flowers.

No, estas no son las flores de ellos. – No, these are not their flowers.

¿Es ese el carro del jefe? – Is that the boss car?

Si, ese es el carro del jefe. – Yes, that is the boss car.

No, ese no es el carro del jefe. – No, that is not the boss car.

¿Son esos los carros del jefe? – Are those the boss' cars?

Si, esos son los carros del jefe. – Yes, those are the boss cars.

No, esos no son los carros del jefe. – No, those are not the boss cars.

¿Es esa la cama de dormir?   - Is that the bed for sleeping?

Si, esa es la cama de dormir. – Yes, that bed is for sleeping.

No, esa no es la cama de dormir. – No, that bed is not for sleeping.

¿Son esas las camas de dormir? – Are those the beds for sleeping?

Si, esas son las camas de dormir. – Yes, those beds are for sleeping.

No, esas no son las camas de dormir. – No, those beds are not for sleeping.

¿Es aquel hombre peligroso? – Is that man over there dangerous?

Si, **aquel** *hombre es peligroso.* – Yes, that man over there is dangerous.

No, **aquel** *hombre no es peligroso.* – No, that man over there is not dangerous.

¿Son aquellos hombres peligrosos? – Are those men over there dangerous?

Si, **aquellos** *hombres son peligrosos.* – Yes, those men over there are dangerous.

No, **aquellos** *hombres no son peligrosos.* – No, those men over there are not dangerous.

¿Es aquella mujer bruta? – Is that woman over there dumb?

Si, **aquella** *mujer es bruta.* – Yes, that woman over is dumb.

No, **aquella** *mujer no es bruta.* – No, that woman over there is not dumb.

¿Son aquellas mujeres brutas? – Are those women over there dumb?

Si, **aquellas** *mujeres son brutas.* – Yes, those women over there are dumb.

No, **aquellas** *mujeres no son brutas.* – No those women over there are not dumb.

Please note that "***esta***" does not have accent, it only takes accent when it is the conjugation of "***Estar***".

Possessive Pronouns – Pronombres posesivos.

Possessive pronouns replace the nouns modified by possessive adjectives. In Spanish, there are different forms of possessive pronouns depending on whether the noun is masculine or feminine, singular or plural. Possessive pronouns are mostly located at the end of a sentence.

Masculine Singular - Masculine Plural

Mío	Míos	Mine
Tuyo	Tuyos	Yours
Suyo	Suyos	Yours / His / Hers
Nuestro	Nuestros	Ours
Suyo	Suyos - Yours / Theirs.	

Since you have already mastered previous section, it is easy for you to learn these ones. Please note that in Spanish they are used with the definite article and without it depending on the sentence.

Remarks:

*Ese carro es **mío**. – That car is mine.

*Esos carros son **míos**. – Those cars are mine.

*Este libro es **tuyo**. – This book is yours.

*Estos libros son **tuyos**. – These books are yours.

Aquel pantalón rojo es **nuestro**. – The red pants over there is ours.

Aquellos pantalones rojos son **nuestros**. – Those red pants over there are ours.

Feminine Singular	Feminine Plural
Mía	Mías- Mine.
Tuya	Tuyas - Yours.
Suya	Suyas - Yours / His / Hers.
Nuestra	Nuestras - Ours.
Suya	Suyas - Yours - Theirs

Remarks:

*Esa cama es **mía**. – That bed is mine.

*Esas camas son **mías**. – Those beds are mine.

*Esta mesa es **tuya**. – This table is yours.

Estas mesas son **tuyas**. – These tables are yours.

Aquella falda roja es **nuestra**. – That red skirt over there is ours.

Aquellas faldas rojas son **nuestras**. – Those red skirts over there are ours.

Since we have already explained "**Suyo** – **Suyos** / **Suya** – **Suyas**" represent five different personal pronouns, we need to make sure people understand us when we speak; therefore, here's what you need to do.

El libro es **suyo** – The book is yours (polite).

El libro es **suyo** – The book is his.

El libro es **suyo** – The book is hers.

El libro es **suyo** – The book is yours (plural).

El libro es **suyo** – The book is theirs.

Since all mean the same in Spanish, we just use "**De** – **of**" plus the personal pronouns to make the difference.

El libro es **de usted** – The book is yours.

El libro es **de él** – The book is his.

El libro es **de ella** – The book is hers.

El libro es **de ustedes** – The book is yours.

El libro es de **ellos (as)** - The book is theirs.

Remember, in Spanish you can use them with the articles as already mentioned.

Masculine Singular	Masculine Plural
El mío	Los míos – Mine.
El tuyo	Los tuyos – Yours.
El suyo	Los suyos – Yours (polite) / His / Hers.
El nuestro	Los nuestros – Ours.

El suyo   Los suyos – Yours (plural), Theirs.

¿De quién es este carro? - Whose this car?

Es el mío. – It is mine.

No, no es el mío. Es el de ella. – No, it is not mime. It is hers.

Este carro es el nuestro. Me encanta nuestro carro. – This car is ours. I love our car.

¿Es este carro el de él? – Is this car his?

Si, este carro es el de él. – Yes, this car is his.

No, este carro no es el de él. – No, this car is not his.

Remember, same rule as above to make the difference between "*Suyo*" and "*De él*". We want people to understand whom we are referring.

Feminine Singular   Feminine Plural

La mía   Las mías – Mine.

La tuya   Las tuyas – Yours.

La suya   Las suyas – Yours (polite) / His / Hers.

La nuestra   Las nuestras – Ours.

La suya   Las suyas – Yours (plural) / Theirs.

¿De quién es esta flor? – Whose this flower?

Es la mía. – It is mine.

No es la mía. – It is not mine.

¿Es esta la casa de ella? – Is this house hers?

Si, esta es la casa de ella. – Yes, this house is hers.

No, esta no es la casa de ella. – No, this house is not hers.

¿Es aquella la madre de Carmen? – Is that one over

there Carmen's mother?

Si, aquella es la madre de Carmen (de ella). O Si, es
la de Carmen (la de ella).

Yes, that one over there is Carmen's mother (hers).
Or Yes, it's Carmen's (hers).

No, aquella no es la madre de Carmen (de ella). O
No, no es la de Carmen (la de ella).

No, that one over there is not Carmen's mother
(hers). Or, no, it not Carmen's (hers).

¿Quién es la chica rubia que está hablando con el
profesor? - Who is the blond girl speaking with the
teacher?

*La chica rubia que está hablando con el profesor es
la hermana de Pedro (de él).* O

Ella es la hermana de Pedro (de él). The blond girl
speaking to the teacher is is Pedro's sister (his). Or
She is Pedro's sister (his).

As you can see, you can substitute the pronoun by
the noun (**De Carmen – De ella**), same with Pedro.

Telling the time – La hora.

Telling the time in Spanish is very easy, since you
already know the numbers by heart. In Spanish we
use the verb "*Ser*" in its conjugation for singular "*Es*"
and plural "*Son*". Use **es** when referring to "one
o'clock" and use **son** when referring to all other hours.

¿Qué hora es? – What time is it?

Es la una en punto (1:00). It is one o'clock.

Es la una y diez (1:10). – It is one ten.

Pasan diez de la una. – It is ten after one.

Es la una y cuarto (1:15). – It is ten and a quarter.

Pasan quince después de la una. – It is fifteen after

one.

Es un cuarto después de la una. – It is a quarter after one.

Es la una y media (1:30). – It is one thirty (literally One and a half).

Es la una y treinta. – It is one thirty.

Pasan treinta después de la una. – It is thirty after one.

Es la una y cuarenta y cinco (1:45). – It is one forty five.

Pasan cuarenta y cinco después de la una. – It is forty five after one.

Falta un cuarto para las dos. – It is a quarter before two.

Es la una y tres cuartos. – It is one and three quarters. (Almost never use).

Since the word *"hora"* is feminine, you need to use all the time the feminine article *"La"* when telling the time.

¿Qué horas son? – What time is it?

Son las tres en punto (3:00) - It is two o'clock.

Son las cuatro en punto (4:00) – It is four o'clock.

Son las cinco y media (5:30) – It is five thirty.

Son las ocho y cuarto (8:15) – It is eight and a quarter.

To differentiate between A.M. and P.M. use the expressions **de la mañana, de la tarde** and **de la noche.**

Son las dos de la tarde (2:00 PM) – It is two in the afternoon.

Son las dos de la mañana (2:00 AM) – It is two in the morning.

Son las ocho de la noche (8:00 PM) – It is eight in the evening.

Son las ocho de la mañana (8:00 AM) – It is eight in the morning.

Son las cinco más o menos (5:00) – It is about five.

Es medio día – It is midday.

Es media noche – It is midnight.

Please note that in some Latin countries we use "*¿Qué hora es?*" At any time of the day. Eventhough we know it is nighttime or any time of the day, we just say *"Qué hora es".* The person answering is the one using the correct form "*Son las 5:00*'.

Some expression related to time. – Expresiones relacioneadas con la hora.

Por la mañana - In the morning (No time in specific)

De la mañana - In the morning (specific time)

Por la tarde - In the afternoon (No time in specific)

De la tarde - In the afternoon (specific time)

Por la noche - In the evening or night (No time in specific)

De la noche - In the evening or night (specific time)

La mañana - Morning

Mañana por la mañana - Tomorrow morning

Pasado mañana - The day after tomorrow

Ayer - Yesterday

Anoche - Last night

La noche anterior, anteanoche, antes de anoche- The night before last

El lunes que viene (el próximo lunes, el lunes

entrante) - Next Monday
La semana que viene (la semana próxima, la semana entrante) - Next week
El año que viene (el año próximo, el año entrante) - Next year
El lunes pasado (el pasado lunes) - Last Monday
La semana pasada - Last week
El año pasado - Last year
Al mediodía - At noon
A la medianoche - At midnight
Alrededor de - Around
De día – Daytime
De noche - Nighttime
Durante el día - During the day
Durante la noche – During the night.
A tiempo - On time
En punto – O'clock
Tarde - Late
Temprano - Early

A Little bit more – Un poco más

Adverbios de frecuencia - Adverbs of Frequency.
Con frecuencia - Regularly
Casi nunca - Seldom
Diariamente - Daily
Cada hora - Every hour / Hourly
Semanalmente - Every week / weekly
Normalmente - Normally
Usualmente - Usually
Ocasionalmente - Occasionally

Anualmente - Every year / Annually
Mensualmente - Every month / Monthly
De vez en cuando - From time to time / Once in a while
Constantemente - Constantly
A veces - Sometimes
Rara vez - Rarely
A menudo - Often
Casi nunca - Almost never
Siempre - Always
Frecuentemente - Frequently
Nunca - Never
Nunca jamás - Never ever

Exercises - Ejercicios
Complete the sentences:

1- Rafael celebra hoy _____ cumpleaños.

2- A la mesa pequeña le pondré _____ mantel que me tejió mamá.

3- Vendrán _____ familiares y

_____amigos allegados.

4- ¿Son _____ hombres peligrosos?

5- Rafael apagará _____ velitas a _____

_____

6- Write a sentence with the word " tu" without accent.

_____

7- Write a sentence with the pronoun " tú" with accent

_____

8- Write a sentence with a demonstrative singular adjective, and underline that adjective.

_____

9- Write a sentence with a demonstrative plural adjective, and underline that adjective.

_____

10- Write three different ways to say 2:30

_____

_____

_____

11- Write two different ways to say 4:15

_____

_____

12- Write two sentences related to time.

_____

Reading Comprehension:

Answer the following questions:

¿A qué hora se levantó Victoria? – At what time did Victoria get up?

¿Quién cortó las flores olorosas? – Who cut the smelly flowers?

¿De quién es la mesa pequeña? – Whose the small table?

¿Por qué se cae la chica de pelo largo? – Why does the long hair girl fall down?

¿Qué ropa usó Victoria? – What clothes did Victoria wear?

Knowledge Base

Republic of Honduras - República de Honduras

Motto: Libre, Soberana e Independiente - Free, Sovereign and Independent

Capital and largest city - Tegucigalpa

Official language - Spanish

Demonym - Honduran (Catracho)

Government - Presidential republic

President - Juan Orlando Hernández

Vice President - Ricardo Álvarez Arias

Population - 2016 estimate - 8 135 999

Currency - Lempira (HNL)

Calling code - +504

Bible Verse - Versículo Bíblico.

Porque de tal manera amó Dios al mundo, que ha dado a su Hijo unigénito, para que todo aquel que en él cree, no se pierda, más tenga vida eterna. **Juan 3:16**

Conclusion

Thank you very much for selecting for your learning experience Teach Yourself Spanish By Yeral Ogando. You have reached the end of Level One, therefore, you are ready to speak Spanish with anyone.

You are now ready for Level Two which you will find by checking out my Amazon page

I encourage you to continue practicing and speaking Spanish at all times, as I have already said Practice makes perfect.

Visit my websites for more information.

Dios te bendiga y nos vemos la próxima vez.

Dr. Yeral Ogando
www.aprendeis.com

BONUS PAGE

Dear Reader,

You need to download the MP3 Audio files to follow this unique method gradually. Please visit our website at:

http://aprendeis.com/spanish-audio1/
The username is "spanish"
The password is "spanish112017"

Just download the Zip File and you are ready to start your learning experience.

If you want to share your experience, comments or possible question, you may always reach me at info@aprendeis.com

Remember:
Reviews can be tough to come by these days, and you, the reader, have the power to make or break a book. If you have the time, share your review or comments with me.

Thank you so much for reading Teach Yourself Spanish and for spending time with me.

In gratitude,
Dr. Yeral E. Ogando

Exercises' answers – Respuesta de los ejercicios

Lesson 1.

1- 27 letters.

2- It sounds like "j"

3- It sounds like "s"

4 Mi nombre es Pedro

5 Hola David.

6- Chico, Chica, Chocolate.

7 Carro, Perro.

Lesson 2.

1- When it ends in "Ar, Er, Ir".

2- Yo amo, tú amas, usted / él / ella ama, nosotros amamos, ustedes / ellos (as) aman.

3- Yo, tú, usted, él, ella.

4- Nosotros, ustedes, ellos (as).

5- También.-   Tampoco

6- 123 Ciento veinte tres

538 quinientos treinta y ocho.

416 cuatrocientos diez y seis.

7 canto

canta

cantamos

cantan

8 camina

caminan

caminas

Lesson 3.
1   las, la, los, el.
2   unos, una, un, unos.
3   M, M, F, F.
4   Inviernos, reyes, domingos, comidas, televisiones
5   Domingo, lunes, martes.
6   invierno, verano, otoño.
7   Hoy es martes y estamos en otoño en el mes de octubre.

Lesson 4.
Mind Game – Juego mental answers:
1.   Quiero conocerte mejor
     Te quiero conocer mejor.
2.   No quiero estudiar hoy, pero quiero beber jugo.
3.   ¿Puedes traer arroz y carne?
¿Puede usted traer arroz y carne?
4.   ¿Puedes darme agua?
     ¿Me puedes dar agua?
     ¿Puede usted darme agua?
     ¿Me puede usted dar agua?
5.   No puedo darte agua, pero puedo darte cerveza.
No te puedo dar agua, pero te puedo dar cerveza.
No puedo darle a usted agua, pero puedo darle a usted cerveza.
No le puedo dar agua, pero le puedo dar cerveza.
6.   Quiero dormir como un bebé mañana.
Mañana quiero dormir como un bebé.

7.   Ella quiere ir al cine, pero él no tiene dinero.

8.   Ellos quieren escribir un email, pero no tienen una computadora.

9.   Queremos estudiar español, pero no tenemos un profesor.

10. No entiendo español muy bien.

¿Puedes hablar inglés?

No comprendo español muy bien. ¿Puede usted hablar inglés?

Exercises – Ejercicios answers:

1. Voy a comer en un restaurante.

Voy a vender mi carro hoy.

Voy a la iglesia con mi hermano.

Si, voy a ir a casa después del trabajo

2. como, comen, comen

corres, corre, corremos

3. duermen, dormimos, duerme.

4. Todos los fines de semana yo como en un restaurante.

Regreso a mi casa después del trabajo

Voy a la iglesia y me duermo bien.

5. De lunes a vierne s nosotros vemos televisión

De lunes a viernes nosotros trabajamos

De lunes a viernes nosotros estudiamos

Lesson 5.

1- Estoy bien, gracias

Estoy muy bien.

Estoy mal

Estoy más o menos

2- soy de… (República Dominicana)

3- La nacionalidad de mi madre es… (Dominicana)
4- Mi padre habla… (Español)
5 Yo soy Marcos
Soy de Italia
Soy italiano y hablo italiano
6 Ella está Feliz
Ella está en la cocina
Ella está bien
7-

Italia	Italiano	Italiano
Francia	Francés	Francés
Japón	Japonés	Japonés
Brasil	Brasileño	Portugués
Turquía	Turco	Turco
Argentina	Argentino	Español

Lesson 6.
1 Quiero comer helado.
A ella le gustaría ir a la iglesia
Las llaves están en la mesa
Hago mi tarea con el libro
Voy a empezar hoy
Mis libros son los azules
Ese carro cuesta 100 pesos
Porque tú no estás conmigo
2 ¿Qué va s a hacer?
¿A dónde quiere ir él?
¿Dónde está la llave?
¿Cómo preparas la comida?
¿Cuándo vienes?
¿Cuál es tu carro?

¿Cuánto cuesta esta manzana?

¿Por qué están ellos alegres?

3   me

     le

     nos

     se

     te

     se

Lesson 7.

1   Yendo, jugando, haciendo, ensuciando, divirtiendo.

2   Me gusta… helado.

     Les gusta… frutas.

     Le gusta…vino.

     Le gusta…cerveza.

     Les gusta…golf.

     Nos gusta…cartas.

Lesson 8.

1   su

2   el

3   Mis… mis.

4   esos

5   Sus… a las10 en punto

6   Me gusta tu libro

7   Tú estás feliz.

8   Este carro es lindo

9   Esas chicas son lindas

10 Dos y treinta

     Dos y media

     Pasan treinta después de las dos

11 Cuatro y quince
  Cuatro y cuarto
  Pasan quince después de las cuatro
12 Son las cinco en punto
  Es la una y media

.

Other books written by Yeral E. Ogando

The Hero Within
Volume One
Awareness
Yeral E. Ogando

El Héroe Dentro de Ti
Volumen Uno
Conciencia
Yeral E. Ogando

The Hero Within
Volume Two
Power
Yeral E. Ogando

The Hero Within
Volume Three
Adventures
Watch for this one next
Yeral E. Ogando

Yeral E. Ogando comes from a very humble origin and continues to be a humble servant of our Lord Almighty; understanding that we are nothing but vessels and the Lord who called us, also sends us to do His work, not our work. Luke 17:10 "So likewise ye, when ye shall have done all those things which are commanded you, say, We are unprofitable servants: we have done that which was our duty to do."

Dr. Ogando was born in the Caribbean, Dominican Republic. He is the beloved father of two beautiful girls "Yeiris & Tiffany"

Jesus brought him to His feet at the age of 16-17. Since then, he has served as Co-pastor, pastor, Bible School teacher, youth counselor, and church planter. He is currently serving as the Secretary for the Dominican Reformed Church as well as the liaison for Haiti and USA.

Fluent in several languages Dr. Ogando is the Creator and owner of an Online Translation Ministry operating since 2007; with Native Christian translators in more than 25 countries.

(www.christian-translation.com),

The most exciting thing about his Translation Ministry is that thousands of people are receiving the Word of God in their native language on a daily basis and hundreds of ministries are able to reach the world through the work of Christian-Translation.com along with his translation network of 17 websites in different languages related to Christian Translation.

.

www.ingramcontent.com/pod-product-compliance
Lightning Source LLC
Chambersburg PA
CBHW071534040426
42452CB00008B/1014